بسم الله الرحمن الرحيم

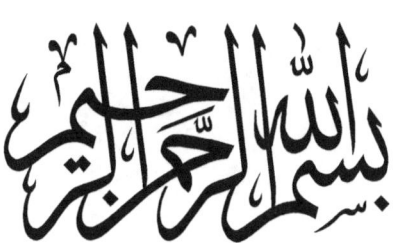

The Branches of Īmān

Imām Qazwīni's رَحِمَهُ ٱللَّهُ abridgement of Imām Bayhaqī's رَحِمَهُ ٱللَّهُ work presented in English with the original Arabic

Imām Abū Qāsim 'Umar bin 'Abdur Raḥmān Qazwīni Ash-Shāfi'ī (d. 699 AH) رَحِمَهُ ٱللَّهُ

The Branches of Īmān

A humble appeal is made to the readers for suggestions/corrections to improve the quality of this publication. May Allāh Taʿālā reward you for this. The author, translators, editors and typesetters humbly request your duʿās for them, their parents, families, asātiza and mashāikh.

Front Page & Secondary Cover Art by Provector (Commercial Licence) via creativemarket.com.

ISBN: 978-0-6482471-6-6

Published by:
Firdaws Academy Press
Level 2, 1830 Sydney Rd, Campbellfield
Victoria 3061, Australia
Web: www.firdawsacademy.org.au/press
Email: publications@firdawsacademy.org.au

Arabic Transliteration Guide

Consonants						Short Vowels	
ء	a/i/u/'	ز	z	ق	q	ـَ	a
ب	b	س	s	ک	k	ـُ	u
ت	t	ش	sh	ل	l	ـِ	i
ث	th	ص	ṣ	م	m	**Long Vowels**	
ج	j	ض	ḍ	ن	n	ا ى	ā
ح	ḥ	ط	ṭ	ه	h	و	ū
خ	kh	ظ	ẓ	و	w	ي	ī
د	d	ع	ʿ	ى	Y	**Diphthongs**	
ذ	dh	غ	gh	ال	al- (article)	ـَو	aw
ر	r	ف	f	ة	a/at	ـَي	ay

Honorifics

عَزَّوَجَلَّ ʿAzza wa Jall– used to praise Allāh Taʿālā – Meaning Glorified and Sublime is He.

ﷺ Sallallāhu ʿalayhi wa sallam — Meaning "May Allāh bless him and give him peace." Used for the Prophet Muḥammed ﷺ.

عَلَيْهَا ٱلسَّلَامُ / عليه السلام / عَلَيْهِمُ ٱلسَّلَامُ ʿAlayhis salām— used following the mention of a prophet of Allāh, their family or angels translated as, "May the peace of Allāh be upon him/her/them."

رضي الله عنه / رضي الله عنهم / رَضِيَ ٱللَّهُ عَنْهَا Raḍiyallāho ʿanhu/ʿanhum/ʿanha —following the name of a companion رضي الله عنه meaning "May Allāh be pleased with him/them/her."

رَحِمَهُ ٱللَّهُ Raḥimahullāh – May Allāh Ta'lā have mercy on him - used for for a pious person.

Contents

Translator's Note 10
Imām al-Qazwīni 12
1. Īmān in Allāh 16
2. Īmān in the Messengers 17
3. Īmān in angels 17
4. Īmān in the Qur'ān and all the revealed books before it 18
5. Īmān in Qadr (Ordaining), that both good and bad is from Allāh 18
6. Īmān in the Last Day 19
7. Īmān in the Resurrection after Death 20
8. Īmān in the Gathering of Mankind to the Standing, after their resurrection from their graves 21
9. Īmān that the abode and refuge of the believers is Jannah, and of the unbelievers, the Fire 22
10. Īmān that it is an obligation to love Allāh Ta'ālā 23
11. Īmān that one must fear Allāh Ta'ālā 25
12. Īmān that one must have hope in Allāh Ta'ālā 27
13. Īmān that one must have tawakkul (rely) on Allāh Ta'ālā 29
14. Īmān in the obligation to love the Prophet ﷺ 31
15. Īmān in the obligation to honour and venerate the Prophet ﷺ 32
16. One's firmness in his Dīn, so that he would rather be cast into the Fire than to leave Islam 33
17. Seeking 'ilm (knowledge) 34
18. Spreading Knowledge 37
19. The Veneration of the Qur'ān Majīd 40
20. Purification 41
21. The Five ṣalāts 43
22. The Zakāt 45
23. Fasting 46
24. I'tikāf 47
25. Ḥajj 48
26. Jihād 50
27. Ribāṭ - Protecting the Islamic Frontiers 51
28. Determination in the face of an enemy, and not fleeing the fight 52
29. Separating and paying the Khums from the spoils of war, to be paid to the Imam or his representative who supervises those who have taken the war booty 53

30. Freeing slaves, as an act of worship...54
31. The kaffārāt which must be paid for criminal offences....................55
32. Fulfilling one's undertakings...56
33. Recounting the blessings of Allāh, and giving the necessary thanks 58
34. Holding one's tongue from unnecessary speech, which includes lying, slandering, backbiting and obscenity...60
35. Holding things in trust for others..61
36. The prohibition of murder and other crimes...................................62
37. Saving oneself from aldultery by adopting chastity.........................63
38. Not appropriating the property of others includes the prohibition of theft, highway robbery, usury (interest) and consuming any money or property to which one is not entitled under Islamic Law......................64
39. The obligation to be scrupulous in matters of food and drink, and to reject what is forbidden...70
40. The prohibition or dislike of certain clothes and eating utensils......75
41. The prohibition of games & amusements which contravene the Shariʿa...76
42. Moderation in expenditure, and the prohibition of consuming wealth unlawfully..77
43. The abandoning of rancour, envy and similar feelings.....................78
44. The sanctity of people's reputations, and the obligation not to cast aspersions upon them...80
45. Ikhlās (sincerety), so that one acts only for Allāh Taʿālā, and avoids all forms of riyā (ostentation)...82
46. Happiness when one has done a good deed, and sorrow when one has commited a sin...84
47. Treating every sin with repentance...85
48. Sacrifices, namely hady (hajj-related sacrifice), and the sacrifices for the ʿĪd and for Aqiqa...86
49. Obedience to those in authority...87
5o. Holding firmly to the Jamāʿa..88
51. Passing judgement between with justice...89
52. Enjoining good, and forbidding evil...91
53. Cooperation in goodness and piety...93
54. Modesty...93
55. Kindness to parents...94
56. Maintaining ties of kinship..95
57. Good character..98

58. Kindness to bondsmen..100
59. The rights upon bondsman 101
60. The rights of children and family 102
61. Keeping the company of pious, loving them, greeting them and shaking their hands, and doing any other thing which would strengthen one's affection for them. 103
62. Responding to the greetings of others 104
63. Visiting the sick 105
64. Praying for any deceased Muslim 106
65. Saying "May Allāh have mercy on you!" to a sneezer 106
66. Keeping the unbelievers and those who act evilly at a distance, and being stern with them..108
67. Honouring one's neighbours...110
68. Honouring guests 111
69. Concealing the sins of others 111
70. Steadfastness in the face of misfortunes and against the desires and delights of the ego 113
71. Renunciation frulll, and short hopes..114
72. Concern Gheera (or Ghayra is the sense of jealousy one feels when someone others look at one'swife) for one's family, and not flirting ..116
73. Turning away from pointless talk...117
74. Generosity and benevolence 118
75. To have mercy for the young and respect for the old 119
76. Reconciling people's differences...120
77. To love for your Muslim brother what you love for yourself, and to hate for him what one would hate for yourself...................................121

مختصر شعب الإيمان

When Allāh Ta'ālā gives you tawfīq to learn 'ilm, know that he wants to give you 'ilm.

Ibn 'Aṭāullāh

Translator's Note

All praise is due to Allāh, our creator, nourisher and provider. Peace and blessings be upon all the prophets and upon the last and final messenger Muḥammed ﷺ and peace and blessings be upon his companions who accepted and propagated Islām to the entire world.

Before you is a translation of Mukhtaṣar Shuʿbul Īmān by Imām Qazwīni رحمه الله. It is an abridgement of the *Branches of Īmān* by Imām Bayhaqī رحمه الله which in reality is a commentary of a single ḥadīth of Rasulullāh ﷺ in which he taught that "Īmān has sixty-odd, or seventy-odd branches, the highest and best of which is to declare that there is no one worthy of worship except Allāh, and the lowest of which is to remove something harmful from the path. And that modesty is a branch of Īmān."

Rasulullāh ﷺ captured and placed in the heart of his umma the beauty of Īmān. There are high branches and low branches. He mentioned three in the hadith but indicated that there are many more.

Imām Bayhaqī رحمه الله endeavoured to compile all the narrations related to Īmān and its branches. This compilation reached six volumes and out of the grasp of the layman and more suited to the research scholars. Imam Qazwīni رحمه الله abridged the original into the short treatise before you which is accessible to all.

When a Muslim strives to become a true and complete Muʾmin, then he must learn and recognise within himself the signs of Īmān or the lack thereof. Allāh Taʿālā and his Messenger ﷺ has told us these signs so we can struggle and pray that he blesses us with a perfect faith before we die.

Īmān cannot be hidden. It will manifest in all aspects of a Muʾmin's or believer's life. The signs will be evident. They will become a light of guidance in the darkness for others.

Branches of Īmān is also a presentation of the fundamental beliefs of Islām and can be utilised for teaching ʿAqīda without resorting to historical polemical debates. I was the encouraged by senior ʿulamā to teach ʿAqīda in adult Islamic studies courses. This is how I came in contact with this book. However, it was difficult to acquire an English version of the text in Australia for the classes. The only translation was an almost thirty-year-old low-quality-scan of the text by Shaykh Abdul Hakim Murad. It also needed to be simplified and be presented to Muslims without the over-translations. Furthermore, the original Arabic was placed along with the English, as this might be helpful for Arabic-speakers or those learning Arabic.

Furthermore, Imām Qazwīni رَحِمَهُ ٱللَّٰهُ masterfully quotes from the greatest ṣāliḥīn of this ummah where required, to show the spiritual significance of these branches.

May Allāh Talaa bestow our unworthy souls with all these branches of Īmān and a means of our salvation. I request the readers for their duʿās and that Allāh Taʿālā accept this work to be solely for his sake. Without His acceptance, all efforts are of no value.

Khalid Shah
Madrasa Islamiyya Kāshiful Uloom
Melbourne, Australia

Imām al-Qazwīni رَحِمَهُ ٱللَّٰهُ

He was the Imām, the judge, the jurist, Imāmmudīn Abū Ma'āli 'Umar ibn Sa'ddudīn Abū Qāsim Abdur Raḥmān bin Shaykh Imāmudīn Abū Hafṣ 'Umar ibn Aḥmed bin Muḥammed al-Qazwīni ash-Shāfi'ī.

He was born in Tabriz in 654 AH, where he acquired his early education. He travelled to many lands especially acquiring 'ilm related to the Shāfi'ī school of thought until he arrived with his brother Jalāluddīn in Damascus and started teaching at numerous madāris. He was appointed as the chief judge after the death of Qāḍi Badruddīn ibn Jamā'a. A post in which he became famous for his integrity and wisdom. His brother was his deputy. He was known for his beautiful character, kindness, leadership and his avoiding of harm to anyone.

He left Damascus at the approach of the Mongols, and travelled to Egypt, where he died at the age of forty-six in 699 AH, only a week after his arrival. He is buried near the grave of Imām Shāfi'ī رَحِمَهُ ٱللَّٰهُ. May Allāh Ta'ālā illuminate his grave and have mercy upon him.

He wrote many beneficial texts such as the present abridgement of Imām Bayhaqī's *Branches of Īmān.*

بِسْمِ ٱللَّهِ ٱلرَّحْمَٰنِ ٱلرَّحِيمِ

In the name of Allāh, the most beneficent and merciful

الْحَمد لله رب الْعَالمين، وَالصَّلَاة وَالسَّلَام على سيد الْمُرسلين، وَخَاتم النبين، وقائد الغر المحجلين، مُحَمَّد الْمَبْعُوث إِلَى الْخلق أَجْمَعِينَ، وعَلى آله الطيبين، وَصَحبه الطاهرين، وَأمته الْمُتَّقِينَ، وأزواجه الطاهرات أُمَّهَات الْمُؤمنِينَ.

All praises are due to Allāh, Lord of the worlds. And blessings and peace be upon the Master of the Messengers, the Seal of the Prophets, the Leader of the beautiful and radiant, Muḥammad, who was sent to all the creatures, and upon his pure family, and pure companions, and Allāh-fearing Ummah, and his pure wives, the Mothers of the Believers.

وَبعد: فقد تكَرر من سيدنَا ومولانا نَادِر بِلَاده، وناصح عباده، وعلامة زَمَانه، وأعجوبة أَوَانه شمس الْمِلَّة وَالدّين، مُحَمَّد بن الْقَاسِم بن أبي الْبَدْر ابْن المليحي الْمزي، الْفَقِيه الْمُحدث الْوَاعِظ - أدام الله توفيقه وَجعل السعادتين صَاحبه ورفيقه - عدَّة مكتوبات من وَاسِط إِلَى بَغْدَاد فِي السُّؤَال عَن عدد شعب الإِيمان حَيْثُ ورد فِي صَحِيح البُخَارِيّ و مُسلم من حَدِيث أبي هُرَيْرَة رَضِي الله عَنهُ عَن النَّبِي صلى الله عَلَيْهِ وَسلم أَنه قَالَ ((الإيمان بضع وَسِتُّونَ أَو بضع وَسَبْعُونَ شُعْبَة أَعْلَاهَا أَو فأرفعها أَو فأفضلها - على اخْتِلَاف الرِّوَايَات - قَول لَا إِلَه إِلَّا الله، وَأَدْنَاهَا إمَاطَة الْأَذَى عَن الطَّرِيق، وَالْحيَاء شُعْبَة من الإيمان)). وَأَنه بصدد إحاطة علمه بتفصيلها عددا، وَتَأَخر الْجَواب لأسباب وعوارض.

And to proceed, our leader and master, who is unique in his land, the well-wisher of Allāh's slaves, the great-scholar of the age and the wonder of the times, the sun of Īmān and Dīn, Muḥammad ibn Qāsim ibn Abū Bakr ibn Maliḥi Mizzi, the jurist, the muḥaddith, the preacher (may Allāh Ta'ālā lengthen his success, and grant him auspiciousness in both the worlds) wrote a number of letters from Wāsiṭ to Baghdād, enquiring about the number of branches of Īmān, pointing out that it is narrated by Abū Hurayra ﷺ in both Ṣaḥīḥ Bukhāri & Ṣaḥīḥ Muslim, that the Prophet ﷺ said: "Īmān has sixty-odd, or seventy-odd branches, the highest and best of which is to declare that there is no one worthy of worship except Allāh, and the lowest of which is to remove something harmful from the path. And that shyness is a branch of Īmān." He wrote that he was detailing these Branches. However, for a variety of reasons, I was unable to provide him with a response.

فحين طَال الزَّمَان وَكثر التكرارا، أحضرت كتاب "شعب الإيمان " للْإِمَام الْحَافِظ الْفَقِيه أبي بكر أَحْمد بن الْحُسَيْن الْبَيْهَقِيّ - سِتّ مجلدات - لأنقلها بذاتها، فَوَجَدتهَا مُتَفَرِّقَة فِي جَمِيعهَا، لم يجمعها أَولا فِي الْخطْبَة وَلَا فِي المجلد الأول، ثمَّ اعتنى بتفاصيل شروحها، لَكِن فرقها فِي جَمِيع الْكتاب. فدعتني الضَّرُورَة إِلَى أَن أجمعها من مجموعها، وأجعلها مختصرة كرؤوس الْمسَائِل، وأقنع باستدلال آيَة من كتاب الله تَعَالَى، أَو بِحَدِيث من أصح مَا رُوِيَ فِيهِ عَن رَسُول الله صلى الله عَلَيْهِ وَسلم، وَرُبمَا زِدْت فِي بعض الشّعب آيَة أَو آيَات، أَو حَدِيثا أَو كَلِمَات، أَو حِكَايَة أَو حكايات، أَو بَيْتا أَو عدَّة أَبْيَات، لم يذكرهَا الْبَيْهَقِيّ. وَقد بوبها سَبْعَة وَسبعين بَابا. أنبأَنَا بجميعها وَجَمِيع الْكتاب الْمَنْقُول هَذَا مِنْهُ جمَاعَة: مِنْهُم الشَّيْخ الْعَالم مُسْند الْعرَاق رشيد الدّين أَبُو عبد الله مُحَمَّد بن عبد الله بن عمر الْمُقْرِئ الْبَغْدَادِيّ بهَا .وَالْقَاضِي تَقِيّ الدّين أَبُو الْفضل سُلَيْمَان بن حَمْزَة بن أَحْمد الْمَقْدِسِي من دمشق .قَالُوا جَمِيعًا: أنبأ الشُّيُوخ الروَاة أَبُو مُحَمَّد الأنجب بن أبي السعادات بن مُحَمَّد بن عبد الرَّحْمَن الجامي. وَأَبُو الْعَبَّاس أَحْمد بن يَعْقُوب بن عبد الله المارستاني. وَأَبُو الْقَاسِم عَليّ ابْن الْحَافِظ أبي الْفرج عبد الرَّحْمَن بن عَليّ بن مُحَمَّد الْجَوْزِيّ. قَالُوا جَمِيعًا: أنبأ أَبُو حَفْص عمر بن أَحْمد بن عمر الزنجاني فِي صفر

سنة اثْنَتَيْنِ وَسِتِّينَ وَخمْس مئة .قَالَ أَخْبرنِي الشَّيْخ أَبُو الْحسن عبيد الله بن مُحَمَّد بن الإِمَام. الْحَافِظ أبي بكر أَحْمد بن الْحُسَيْن بن عَليّ الْبَيْهَقِيّ .قَالَ: أَخْبرنِي جدي الإِمَام أَبُو بكر .ح وأخبرناها عَالِيا عددا مُسْند الْوَقْت أَبُو الْحسن عَليّ بن أَحْمد بن عبد الْوَاحِد الْمَقْدِسِي إجَازَة عَامَّة إِن لم تكن خَاصَّة. قَالَ: أخبرنَا حَافظ بَغْدَاد أَبُو الْفرج عبد الرَّحْمَن بن عَليّ بن مُحَمَّد الْجَوْزِيّ، ومفتي خُرَاسَان أَبُو سعد عبد الله بن أَحْمد بن عمر الصفار النَّيْسَابُورِي إجَازَة خَاصَّة .قَالَا: أنبأنَا كَذَلِك أَبُو الْقَاسِم زَاهِر بن طَاهِر بن مُحَمَّد الشحامي وَجَمَاعَة .قَالُوا: أنبأنَا الإِمَام الْحَافِظ أَبُو بكر أَحْمد بن الْحُسَيْن الْبَيْهَقِيّ رَحمَه الله عَلَيْهِم أَجْمَعِينَ قَالَ: مُخْتَصر شعب الايمان للبيهقي.

As time passed, and the request was repeated many times, I acquired the six volumes of the *The Branches of Īmān* by the Imām, the Ḥāfiẓ, The Jurist, Abū Bakr Aḥmad bin al-Ḥusayn al-Bayhaqī in order to copy out these 'branches'. However, I discovered that they were scattered throughout the work, and were not mentioned all together in its introduction or in the first volume, and that the author, by providing a great many details and interpretations, had dispersed them throughout the book. I therefore found it necessary to compile them into one summary and to use them as headings for the most important subjects, quoting only one verse from Allāh's Book, and one of the most authentic aḥādith of His Messenger ﷺ. For some of the 'Branches' an extra verse or two were added, or an extra hadith or a few words of explanation, or an anecdote, or a verse of poetry, which were not used by al-Bayhaqī in the original work. The branches were divided into seventy-seven chapters accordingly.

The original Arabic contains a chain of narration for the original book from the author until Imām Bayhaqī. It has been omitted for the sake of brevity.

The Branches of Īmān

الأول من شعب الإيمان

الإيمان بِالله عز وَجل لقَوْله تَعَالَى ﴿والمؤمنون كُلٌّ آمَنَ بِالله﴾ وَلقَوْله تَعَالَى ﴿يَا أَيهَا الَّذين آمَنُوا آمِنُوا بِالله﴾.

ثمَّ سَاق فِيهِ حَدِيث أبي هُرَيْرَة رَضِي الله عَنهُ الْمُتَّفق عَلَيْهِ فِي الصَّحِيحَيْنِ ((أُمرت أَنْ أُقَاتِل النَّاس حَتَّى يقُولُوا لَا إِله الا الله. فَمن قَالَ لَا إِلَه إِلَّا الله فقد عَصَمَ مِنِّي نَفْسَهُ وَمَالَهُ إِلَّا بِحقِّهِ وَحِسَابُهُ على الله تَعَالَى)).

وَحَدِيث عُثْمَان بن عَفَّان رَضِي الله عَنهُ فِي صَحِيح مسلم ((من مَاتَ وَهُوَ يَعْلَمُ أَنْ لَا إِله الا الله دَخَلَ الْجنَّة)).

1. Īmān in Allāh ﷻ

Allāh Taʿālā says "And the believers; all have īmān in Allāh",[1] and "O you who believe, have īmān in Allāh!"[2]
Also, in a ḥadīth narrated by Abū Hurayra ؓ, as *agreed upon*[3] in the Ṣaḥīḥayn (i.e. Ṣaḥīḥ Bukhāri & Ṣaḥīḥ Muslim) that Rasulullāh ﷺ said "I have been commanded to fight until people say, *lā-ilāha il-lal-lāhu* (there is none worthy of worship except Allāh). When they do so, their lives and property become inviolable to me, except in matters of justice[4], and it is Allāh who shall call them to account."
In Ṣaḥīḥ Muslim, it is related in another ḥadīth, narrated by ʿUthmān bin ʿAffān ؓ: "Whoever dies knowing that there is none worthy of worship except Allāh, shall enter Jannah."

---

[1] Baqarah, 285.
[2] Nisā, 136.
[3] *Agreed upon* means that both Imām Bukhāri and Imām Muslim have considered this ḥadīth to be ṣaḥīḥ.
[4] Justice means the application of capital punishment by a judge for a deserving crime e.g. murder.

الثاني من شعب الإيمان

الإيمان برسل الله عز وجل صلى الله عَلَيْهِم أَجْمَعِينَ وَسَلَّمَ لقَوْله تَعَالَى ﴿والمؤمنون كُلٌّ آمَنَ بِالله وَمَلَائِكَتِه وَكُتُبِهِ وَرُسُلِهِ﴾.

وَلِحَدِيث عُمَرَ بن الْخَطَّابِ رَضِي الله عَنهُ فِي الصَّحِيحَيْنِ فِي سُؤال جِبْرِيلَ عَلَيْهِ السَّلَام «الإيمانُ أَنْ تُؤْمِنَ بِالله وَمَلَائِكَتِهِ وَكُتُبِهِ وَرُسُلِهِ».

2. Īmān in the Messengers عَلَيْهِمُ السَّلَامُ

Allāh Taʿālā says: *And the believers; all have īmān in Allāh, and His angels, and His books, and His messengers.*[5] In the ḥadīth of ʿUmar ibn al-Khattāb ﷺ as narrated in the Ṣaḥīḥayn that the Prophet ﷺ said when replying to Jibrīl: "Īmān is to believe in Allāh, and His angels, and His books, and His messengers."

الثالث من شعب الإيمان

الإيمان بِالْمَلَائِكَةِ لِلْآيَةِ والْحَدِيث الْمَذْكُورين.

3. Īmān in angels

This is mentioned in the previous ayat and ḥadīth.

الرابع من شعب الإيمان

الإيمان بِالْقُرْآنِ وَجَمِيع الْكتب الْمنزلَة قبله لقَوْله تَعَالَى ﴿يَا أَيُّهَا الَّذِيْنَ آمَنُوْا آمِنُوا بِالله وَرَسُوْلِهِ وَالْكِتَابِ الَّذِي نَزَّلَ عَلَى رَسُولِهِ وَالْكِتَابِ الَّذِي أُنْزِلَ مِنْ قَبْلُ﴾ وللآية والْحَدِيث الْمَذْكُورَيْنِ أيضا.

---

[5] Baqarah, 285.

4. Īmān in the Qur'ān and all the revealed books before it

Allāh Ta'ālā says: "O you who believe! Have īmān in Allāh, and His Messenger, the Book which he revealed to His Messenger and the Book which was revealed before it."[6]
This (branch) is also mentioned in the previous ayat and ḥadīth.

الخامس من شعب الإيمان

الإيمان بِأَن الْقدر خَيره وشرّه من الله عز وَجل لقَوْله تَعَالَى ﴿قُلْ كُلٌّ مِنْ عِنْدِ اللهِ﴾.

وَلِحَدِيث أبي هُرَيْرَة رَضِي الله عَنهُ فِي الصَّحِيحَيْنِ ((إحْتَجَّ آدَمُ وَمُوْسَى فَقَالَ مُوسَى يَا آدَمُ أَنْتَ أَبُوْنَا خَيَّبْتَنَا وَأَخْرَجْتَنَا مِنْ الْجَنَّة. فَقَالَ لَهُ آدَمُ يَا مُوسَى إصْطَفَاكَ اللهُ بِكَلَامِهِ وَخَطَّ لَكَ التَّوْرَاةَ بِيَدِهِ أَتَلُوْمُنِيْ عَلَى أَمْرٍ قَدَّرَهُ الله عَليّ قَبْل أن يَخْلُقَنِي بِأَرْبَعِينَ سنة. قَالَ فَحَجَّ آدمُ مُوسَى)).

وَبِالْإِسْنَادِ الْمَذْكُور أنشدنا الإِمَام أبو بكر الْبَيْهَقِيّ قَالَ أنشدني أبو الفوارس جُنَيْد بن احْمَد الطَّبَرِيّ:

العَبْد ذُو ضَجَرٍ والرَّبُّ ذُو قَدَرٍ ... وَالدَّهْرُ ذُو دُوَلٍ والرزق مقسومُ
وَالْخَيْرُ أَجْمَعُ فِيمَا اخْتَار خَالقُنَا ... وَفِي إخْتِيَارِ سِوَاهُ اللّومُ والشُّومُ.

5. Īmān in Qadr (Ordaining), that both good and bad is from Allāh ﷻ

Allāh Ta'ālā says: "say, all things are from Allāh".[7] In a ḥadīth of Abū Hurayra ؓ, the Prophet ﷺ said, as narrated in the Ṣaḥīḥayn tha "Ādam ؑ and Mūsa ؑ once disputed. Mūsa ؑ said, 'O

---

[6] Nisā, 136.
[7] Nisā, 78.

Ādam! You are our father, but you let us down, and expelled us from the Jannah!' And Ādam عليه السلام replied, 'O Mūsa! Allāh chose you to receive His words, and wrote the Torah for you with His own hand. Do you blame me for something which Allāh had destined for me forty years before He created me?' Therefore, Ādam عليه السلام prevailed over Mūsa عليه السلام."

Imām Abū Bakr Bayhaqī quotes Abul Fawāris Junayd ibn Aḥmad Ṭabari that he recited the following couplets:

The slave is disgruntled, but Allāh has preordained
Time changes all, man's provisions are decreed
All good lies in what our Creator has chosen
To try to follow something else is blameworthy and a misfortune.

السادس من شعب الإيمان

الإيمان بِالْيَوْمِ الآخر لقَوْل الله تَعَالَى ﴿قَاتلُوا الَّذين لَا يُؤمنُونَ بِالله وَلَا بِالْيَوْمِ الآخِرِ﴾. قَالَ الْحَلِيمِيّ وَمَعْنَاهُ التَّصْدِيق بِأَن لِأَيّام الدُّنْيَا آخرا، وَأَنَّهَا منقضية، وَهَذَا الْعَالم منقضٍ يوْمًا مَا، فَفِي الإعْتِرَاف بانتفائه، إعْتِرَاف بابتدائه، إذ الْقَدِيم لَا يَفنَي وَلَا يتَغَيَّر.

وفِي الصَّحِيحَيْنِ من حَدِيث أبي هُرَيْرَة رَضِي الله عَنهُ ((وَالَّذِي نفس مُحَمَّد بِيَدِهِ لَتَقُوْمَنَّ السَّاعَةُ وَثوْبُهُمَا بَيْنَهُمَا لَا يَتَبَايَعَانِهِ وَلَا يَطْوِيَانِهِ وَلَتَقُومَنَّ السَّاعَةُ وَقد إنْصَرف الرَّجُلُ بِلَبَنِ لِقحَتِهِ مِنْ تحتِهَا وَقد رَفَعَ أَكْلَتَهُ إلَى فِيهِ لَا يطْعَمُهَا...)) الحَدِيث.

6. Īmān in the Last Day

Allāh Taʿālā says: "Fight those who do not believe in Allāh and the Last Day".[8] Regarding this verse, Ḥalīmi said "this means to believe that the days of this world shall come to an end, and that every day

[8] Tawba, 291.

that passes uses up some of the remaining span. In addition, to confess that there shall be an end obliges us to confess that there has been a beginning, since that which is without a beginning (can only only refer to Allāh Taʿālā) cannot pass away or change.
It is narrated in the Ṣaḥīḥayn by Abū Hurayra ﵁ that theProphet ﷺ said "By Him in Whose hand is the soul of Muḥammed, the Hour shall surely come. The Hour will be established (so suddenly) that two persons spreading a garment between them will not be able to finish their bargain, nor will they be able to fold it up. The Hour will be established (so suddenly) while a man is lifting the milk from his she-camel. However, he will not be able to raise it to his mouth to drink it in time..."

السابع من شعب الإيمان

الإيمان بِالْبَعْثِ بعد الْمَوْت لقَوْله تَعَالَى ﴿زَعَمَ الَّذِينَ كَفَرُوٓا أَن لَّن يُبْعَثُوا قُلْ بَلَىٰ وَرَبِّي لَتُبْعَثُنَّ﴾ وَلقَوْله تَعَالَى ﴿قُلِ اللَّهُ يُحْيِيكُمْ ثُمَّ يُمِيتُكُمْ ثُمَّ يَجْمَعُكُمْ إِلَىٰ يَوْمِ الْقِيَامَةِ لَا رَيْبَ فِيهِ﴾.

وَلِحَدِيث عُمَرَ بن الْخَطّاب رَضِي الله عَنهُ فِي الصَّحِيح فِي حَدِيث الإيمان: «الإيمانُ أَن تُؤْمِنَ بِاللهِ وَمَلَائِكَتِهِ وَكُتُبِهِ وَرُسُلِهِ وَبِالْبَعْثِ مِنْ بَعْدِ الْمَوْتِ، وَبِالْقَدَرِ كُلِّهِ».

7. Īmān in the Resurrection after Death

Allāh Taʿālā says: "The disbelievers claim that they will not be resurrected. Say, by my Lord, you shall most surely be resurrected!"[9] And He says: "Say, Allāh gives you life, and then gives you death, and shall then gather you together on the Day of

[9] Taghābun, 7.

Reserruction in which there is no doubt." [10]
In a ḥadīth narrated by ʿUmar ibn Khattāb ﷺ in the Ṣaḥīḥ (of Imām Bukhāri) "Īmān is that you should believe in Allāh, and His angels, and His books, and His messengers, and in the Resurrection after death, and in the entirety of Qadr."

الثّامِن من شعب الإيمان

الإيمان بحشر النَّاس بَعْدَمَا يبعثون من قُبُورهم إلى الْموقف لقَوْله تَعَالَى ﴿أَلَا يَظُنُّ أُولَئِكَ أَنَّهُمْ مَبْعُوْثُوْنَ لِيَوْمٍ عَظِيْمٍ يَوْمَ يَقُوْمُ النَّاسُ لِرَبِّ الْعَالَمِيْنَ﴾.
وَلِحَدِيث عبدِ اللهِ بن عُمَرَ رَضِي الله عَنْهُمَا فِي صَحِيح مُسلم ((يَقُوْمُ النَّاسُ لِرَبِّ الْعَالَمِيْنَ حَتَّى يَغِيْبَ أَحَدُهُمْ فِيْ رَشْحِهِ إِلَى أَنْصَافِ أُذُنَيْهِ)).

8. Īmān in the Gathering of Mankind to the Standing[11], after their resurrection from their graves

Allāh Taʿālā says: "Do they not believe that they shall be resurrected to a mighty day, a day on which all people shall stand before the Lord of the worlds."
The Prophet ﷺ said, in the ḥadīth of Ibn ʿUmar ﷺ related in Ṣaḥīḥ Muslim that "Mankind shall stand before the Lord of the worlds until some people shall be submerged to their ears in their own sweat."

التَّاسِع من شعب الإيمان

الإيمان بِأَن دَار الْمُؤمنِينَ ومأواهم الْجنَّة وَدَار الْكَافرين ومأواهم النَّار لقَوْله تَعَالَى ﴿بَلَى مَنْ كَسَبَ سَيِّئَةً وَأَحَاطَتْ بِهِ خَطِيْئَتُهُ فَأُولَئِكَ أَصْحَابُ النَّارِ هُمْ فِيْهَا

---

[10] Jāthiyah, 26.
[11] Standing refers standing at the Mahshar or the place where people will gather so as to be questioned.

خَالِدُونَ وَالَّذين آمَنُوا وَعمِلُوا الصَّالِحَاتِ أُولَئِكَ أَصْحَابُ الْجَنَّةِ هم فِيهَا خَالدُونَ﴾.

وَلِحَدِيث إبْن عُمَرَ رَضِي الله عَنْهُمَا فِي الصَّحِيحَيْنِ ((إنَّ أحَدَكُمْ إذَا مَاتَ عُرِضَ عَلَيْهِ مَقْعَدَهُ بِالْغَدَاةِ وَالعَشِيِّ. وَإِنْ كَانَ مِنْ أَهْلِ الْجَنَّةِ فَمِنْ أَهْلِ الْجَنَّةِ وَإِنْ كَانَ مِنْ أَهْلِ النَّارِ فَمِنْ أَهْلِ النَّار. يُقَال هَذَا مَقْعَدُكَ حَتَّى يَبْعَثَكَ اللهُ تَعَالَى إلَيْهِ يَوْمَ الْقِيَامَةِ)).

9. Īmān that the abode and refuge of the believers is Jannah, and of the unbelievers, the Fire

Allāh Ta'ālā says: "Yes, whoever earns evil and his sin has encompassed him - those are the companions of the Fire; they will abide therein eternally. But they who believe and do righteous deeds - those are the companions of Jannah; they will abide therein eternally."[12]

The Prophet ﷺ said, in the ḥadīth of Ibn 'Umar ؓ related by Bukhāri and Muslim, "When each one of you dies, his place is shown to him morning and night. If he is to be one of the people of Jannah, then it is in Jannah, and if he is to be one of the people of the Fire, then it is the Fire. And he shall be told, 'This is your place until Allāh resurrects you unto Him on the Day of Reserruction'."

الْعَاشِر من شعب الإيمان

الإيمان بِوُجُوب محبَّة الله عز وَجل لقَوْله تَعَالَى ﴿وَمِنَ النَّاسِ مَنْ يتَّخِذُ مِنْ دُوْنِ اللهِ أَنْدَادًا يُحِبُّوْنَهُمْ كَحُبِّ اللهِ وَالَّذِيْنَ آمَنُوْا أَشَدُّ حُبًّا لِلَّهِ﴾.

وَلِحَدِيث أنس بن مَالك رَضِي الله عَنهُ فِي الصَّحِيحَيْنِ ((ثَلَاثٌ مَنْ كُنَّ فِيهِ وَجَدَ

[12] Baqarah, 81.

بِهِنَّ حَلَاوَةَ الإِيْمَانِ، وَأَنْ يَكُوْنَ اللهُ وَرَسُولُهُ أَحَبَّ إِلَيْهِ مِمَّا سِوَاهُمَا وَأَنْ يُحِبَّ الْمَرْءُ لَا يُحِبُّهُ إلا لِلّهِ وَأَنْ يَكْرَهَ أَنْ يَعُوْدَ فِيْ الْكُفْرِ بَعْدَ أَنْ أَنْقَذَهُ اللهُ مِنْهُ كَمَا يَكْرَهُ أَنْ تُوْقَدَ لَهُ نَارٌ فَيُقْذَفَ فِيهَا)).

وَبِهِ أَنبأَنَا الْبَيْهَقِيّ قَالَ سَمِعت أَبَا عبد الرَّحْمَن السّلميّ يَقُول سَمِعتُ أَبَا نضر الطوسي يَقُول سَمِعت جَعْفَر الْخُلْدِيّ يَقُول سَمِعت الْجُنَيْد يَقُول قَالَ رجل لسريّ السَّقطِي كَيفَ أَنْت فَأَنْشَأَ يَقُول:

مَن لَم يَبِتْ وَالْحُبُّ حَشْوُ فُؤَادِهِ ... لَمْ يَدْرِ كَيفَ تُفَتَّتْ الاكبادُ.

وَبِه أنبأ أَبُو عبد الرَّحْمَن السّلميّ قَالَ سَمِعت أَبَا نصر مُحَمَّد بن إِسمَاعِيل قَالَ سَمِعت أَبَا الْقَاسِم الرَّازِيّ الْوَاعِظ قَالَ سَمِعت أَبَا دُجَانَة يَقُول كَانَت رَابِعَة إِذا غلب عَلَيْهَا حَال الْحُبّ تَقول:

تَعْصِي الإِلهَ وَأَنت تُظْهِرَ حُبَّهُ ... هَذَا مُحَال فِي الفِعَالِ بديعُ

لَو كَانَ حُبُّكَ صَادِقا لأَطَعْتَهُ ... إِنَّ الْمُحِبَّ لِمَنْ أَحَبَّ مُطِيعُ.

10. Īmān that it is an obligation to love Allāh Taʿālā

Allāh Taʿālā says "And among the people are those who take other than Allāh as equals (to Him). They love them as they (should) love Allāh. But those who have Īmān are stronger in love for Allāh." [13]
It is narrated in the Ṣaḥīḥayn by Anas ibn Mālik ؓ that the Prophet ﷺ said: "There are three qualities whoever has them, will taste the sweetness of Īmān: To love Allāh and His Messenger ﷺ more than anyone else; to love a slave (of Allāh) only for (the sake of) Allāh; and to hate returning to kufr after Allāh has saved him from it as he would hate to be thrown into a blazing fire."
Al-Sari al-Saqati was once asked, "How are you?" and he recited the following couplet:

[13] Baqarah, 165.

Whoever does not feel love filling his breast,
Cannot know how hearts can be torn apart.

Abū Dujāna said that Rābiʿa ʿAdawiyya, would say, when the state of love of Allāh overwhelmed her:

You disobey Allāh and express that you love Him;
This is impossible, and a bizarre affair!
If your love was true, you would obey Him;
For lovers always obey the ones they love.

الْحَادِي عشر من شعب الإيمان

الإيمان بِوُجُوب الْخَوْف من الله عزّ وَجلّ لقَوْله تَعَالَى ﴿فَلَا تَخَافُوْهُمْ وَخَافُوْنِ إِن كُنْتُم مُؤمنين﴾ وَقَوله تَعَالَى ﴿فَلَا تَخْشَوُا النَّاسَ وَاخْشَوْنِ﴾ وَقَوله تَعَالَى ﴿وَإِيَّايَ فَارْهَبُوْنِ﴾ وَقَوله تَعَالَى ﴿وَهُمْ مِنْ خَشْيَتِهِ مُشْفِقُوْنَ﴾ وَقَوله تَعَالَى ﴿وَيَدْعُوْنَنَا رَغَبًا وَرَهَبًا وَكَانُوْا لَنَا خَاشِعِيْنَ﴾ وَقَوله تَعَالَى ﴿وَيَخْشَوْنَ رَبَّهُمْ وَيَخَافُونَ سُوْءَ الْحِسَابِ﴾ وَقَوله تَعَالَى ﴿وَلِمَنْ خَافَ مَقَامَ رَبِّهِ جَنَّتَانِ﴾ وَقَوله تَعَالَى ﴿ذَلِكَ لِمَنْ خَافَ مَقَامِيْ وَخَافَ وَعِيْدِ﴾.

وَلِحَدِيث عدي بن حَاتِم رَضِي الله عَنهُ فِي الصَّحِيحَيْنِ ((إتَّقُوا النَّارَ وَلَو بِشِقِّ تَمْرَةٍ)).

وَلِحَدِيث أَنَسٍ رَضِي اللهُ عَنهُ فِيْهِمَا ((لَوْ تَعْلَمُونَ مَا أَعْلَمُ لَضَحِكْتُمْ قَلِيْلًا وَلَبَكَيْتُمْ كَثِيْرًا)).

وعاتب رجل بعض إخوانه على طول بكائه فبكى ثمَّ قَالَ:

بَكَيْت على الذُّنوب لِعُظْمِ جُرْمِي ... وَحُقَّ لِكُلِّ مَنْ يَعْصِي الْبُكَاءُ
فَلَوْ كَانَ الْبكاءُ يَرُدُّ هَمِّيْ ... لَاَسْعَدَتِ الدُّمُوعَ مَعًا دِمَاءُ.

وَكَانَ عمر بن عبد الْعَزِيز لَا يَجِفُّ فوه من هَذَا الْبَيْت:

وَلَا خير فِي عَيْش إمرِىءٍ لم يكن لَهُ ... من الله فِي دَار الْقرارِ نصيبُ

وَسمع أَبُو الْفَتْح الْبَغْدَادِيّ هاتفا يَهْتِف بالشُّونِيْزِيَّة:

وَكَيْفَ تَنَامُ الْعَيْنُ وَهِيَ قَرِيْرَةٌ ... وَلَمْ تَدْرِ فِيْ أَيِّ المَحَلَّيْنِ تَنْزِلُ

فَذهب عَنهُ النوم.

11. Īmān that one must fear Allāh Taʿālā

Allāh Taʿālā says: "So fear them not, but fear Me, if you are (indeed) believers"[14] and also "So do not fear the people but fear Me",[15] and: "And be afraid of (only) Me",[16] and: "And they, from fear of Him, are apprehensive.",[17] and: "They used to hasten to good deeds and supplicate Us in hope and fear, and they were to Us humbly submissive.",[18] and: "They fear their Lord and are afraid of the evil of (their) account",[19] and: "But for he who has feared the position of his Lord are two gardens",[20] and: "That is for he who fears My position and fears My threat."[21]

It is narrated in the Ṣaḥīḥayn by ʿAdiy ibn Ḥātim ؓ that the Prophet ﷺ said "Ward off the Fire, even if only with half a date (in charity)."

It is narrated (in Bukhāri) by Anas ؓ that the Prophet ﷺ said, "If you knew what I know you would laugh little and weep much."

A man once reproached one of his friends for weeping frequently. But he only wept again, and replied:

I weep because my sins are many
All who sin should weep
If weeping could lessen my grief
I would cry till I wept tears of blood.

ʿUmar ibn ʿAbdul ʿAzīz used to repeat the following couplet

---

[14] Āl ʿImrān, 175.
[15] Māida, 44.
[16] Baqarah, 40.
[17] Ambiyā, 28.
[18] Ambiyā, 90.
[19] Raʿd, 21.
[20] Raḥmān, 46.
[21] Ibrāhīm, 14.

repeatedly:

There is no good in the life of a man
For whom Allāh has appointed no share in the hereafter

Abū Fatḥ al-Baghdādi once heard a voice in the cemetery of Shuniziya, which said:

How could anyone sleep soundly who does not know
in which of the two abodes he shall dwell?

Afterwards, he found himself unable to sleep at all.

الثَّانِي عشر من شعب الإيمان

الإيمان بِوُجُوب الرَّجَاء من الله عز وَجل لقَوْله تَعَالَى ﴿يَرْجُوْنَ رَحْمَتَهُ وَيَخَافُوْنَ عَذَابَهُ إِنَّ عَذَابَ رَبِّكَ كَانَ مَحْذُوْرًا﴾ وَقول الله تَعَالَى ﴿وادعُوْهُ خَوْفًا وَطَمَعًا إِنَّ رَحْمَتَ اللهِ قَرِيْبٌ مِنَ الْمُحْسِنِينَ﴾ وَقول الله تَعَالَى ﴿قُلْ يَا عِبَادِيَ الَّذِيْنَ أَسْرَفُوْا عَلَى أَنْفُسِهِمْ لَا تَقْنَطُوْا مِنْ رَحْمَةِ اللهِ إِنَّ اللهَ يَغْفِرُ الذُّنُوْبَ جَمِيْعًا إِنَّهُ هُوَ الْغَفُوْرُ الرَّحِيْمُ﴾ وَقول الله تَعَالَى ﴿إِنَّ اللهَ لَا يَغْفِرُ أَنْ يُشْرَكَ بِهِ وَيَغْفِرُ مَا دُوْنَ ذَلِكَ لِمَنْ يَشَاءُ﴾.

وَلِحَدِيث أبي هُرَيْرَة رَضِي الله عَنهُ فِي الصَّحِيحَيْنِ «لَوْ يَعْلَمُ الْمُؤْمِنُ مَا عِنْدَ اللهِ مِنْ الْعُقُوْبَةِ مَا طَمِعَ بِجَنَّتِهِ أَحَدٌ وَلَو يَعْلَمُ الْكَافِرُ مَا عِنْدَ اللهِ مِنَ الرَّحْمَةِ مَا قَنَطَ مِنْ جَنَّتِهِ أَحَدٌ».

وَلِحَدِيث جَابر رَضِي الله عَنهُ فِي صَحِيح مُسلم «لَا يَمُوْتَنَّ أَحَدُكُمْ إِلَّا وَهُوَ يُحْسِنُ الظَّنَّ بِاللهِ عَزَّ وَجَلَّ».

وَحَدِيث أبي هُرَيْرَة فِي الصَّحِيحَيْنِ «يَقُوْلُ اللهُ عَزَّ وَجَلَّ أَنَا عِنْدَ ظَنِّ عَبْدِي بِي، وَأَنَا مَعَهُ حِينَ يَذْكُرُنِي» وَذكر الحَدِيث.

وَأنْشد أَبُو عُثْمَان سعيد بن إسماعيل:

مَا بَالُ دِيْنِكَ تَرْضَى أَنْ تُدَنِّسَهُ ... وَإِنَّ ثَوْبَكَ مغسولٌ مِنَ الدَّنَسِ

تَرْجُوْ النَّجَاةَ وَلَمْ تَسْلُكْ مَسَالِكَهَا ... إِنَّ السَّفِينَةَ لَا تَجْرِي عَلَى الْيَبَسِ

12. Īmān that one must have hope in Allāh Ta'ālā

Allāh Ta'ālā says: "They hope for His mercy and fear His punishment",[22] and: "Indeed, the mercy of Allāh is near to the doers of good",[23] and: "Say, 'O My servants who have transgressed against themselves (by sinning), do not despair of the mercy of Allāh. Indeed, Allāh forgives all sins. Indeed, it is He who is the Forgiving, the Merciful",[24] and: "Indeed, Allāh does not forgive association with Him, but He forgives what is less than that for whom He wills".[25]

It is narrated in the Ṣaḥīḥayn by Abū Hurayra ﷺ that the Prophet ﷺ said "Were the believers only to know what punishment Allāh has in store, none would hope for His Jannah. And were the unbelievers to know what mercy Allāh has in store, none would despair of His Jannah."

It is narrated in Ṣaḥīḥ Muslim by Abū Hurayra ﷺ that the Prophet ﷺ said: "None should die without thinking well of Allāh."

It is also narrated in the Ṣaḥīḥayn by Abū Hurayra ﷺ that the Prophet ﷺ said "Allāh Ta'ālā declares, 'I am as My slave thinks Me to be, and I am with him when he remembers Me'."

Sa'īd ibn Ismāil recited the following couplets:

Why are you prepared to dirty your Dīn
although your clothes are clean and white?
You hope for salvation, but flee from its paths;
A ship cannot sail on dry land!

---

[22] Isrā, 57.
[23] A'rāf, 56.
[24] Zumar, 53.
[25] Nisā, 48.

الثَّالِث عشر من شعب الإيمان

الإيمان يُوجب التَّوكُّل على الله عز وَجل لقَوْله تعَالَى ﴿وعَلى اللهِ فَلْيَتوَكَّلِ الْمُؤْمِنُونَ﴾ وَقَوله تَعَالَى ﴿حَسْبُنَا اللهُ وَنِعْمَ الْوَكِيْلُ﴾ وَقَوله تَعَالَى ﴿وعَلَى اللهِ فَتوَكَّلُوْا إِنْ كُنْتُمْ مُؤْمِنِيْنَ﴾ وَقَوله تَعَالَى ﴿وَمَنْ يَتوَكَّلْ عَلَى اللهِ فَهُوَ حَسْبُهُ إِنَّ اللهَ بَالِغُ أَمْرِهِ﴾.

وَلِحَدِيث إبْن عَبَّاس رَضِي الله عَنْهُمَا فِي الصَّحِيحَيْنِ فِي سُؤال أَصْحَابه لَهُ عَن السّبْعين ألفًا الَّذين يَدْخلُونَ الْجنَّة يُرْزقُونَ فِيهَا بِغَيْر حِسَابٍ فِي حَدِيثٍ طَوِيْلٍ. فَقَالَ رَسُولُ الله صلى الله عَلَيْهِ وَسلم ((هُمُ الَّذين لَا يَكْتَوُوْنَ وَلَا يَسْتَرقون وَلَا يَتَطَيَّرُونَ وعَلى رَبِّهِمْ يَتَوَكَّلُونَ. فَقَامَ عُكَّاشَةُ بنُ مِحْصَن الأَسَدِي رَضِي الله عَنهُ فَقَالَ أَنا مِنْهُم يَا رَسُول الله؟ فَقَالَ أَنْت مِنْهُم. ثمَّ قَامَ رجلٌ آخَرُ فَقَالَ أَنا مِنْهُم؟ يَا رَسُول الله. فَقَالَ سَبَقَك بهَا عُكَّاشَةُ)). وَجُمْلَة التَّوكُّل تَفْوِيضُ الأمر إلى الله تَعَالَى والثقةُ بِهِ مَعَ مَا قُدِّر لَهُ من التَّسَبُّب.

فَفِي الصَّحِيحَيْنِ أيضا من حَدِيث الزبير رَضِي الله عَنهُ ((لَأن يَأْخُذَ أَحَدُكُمْ حَبْلَهُ ثُمَّ يَأْتِي الْجَبَل فَيَأْتِي بِحُزْمَةٍ مِنْ حَطب عَلَى ظَهْرِهِ فَيَبِيْعَهَا فَيَسْتَغْنِيَ بِهَا خَيْرٌ لَهُ مِنْ أَنْ يَسْأَلَ النَّاسَ أَعْطَوْهُ أَو مَنَعُوْهُ)).

وَفِي صَحِيح البُخَارِيّ من حَدِيث الْمِقْدَام بن معدي كرب رَضِي الله عَنهُ ((مَا أَكَلَ أَحَدٌ طَعَامًا قَطُّ خَيْرًا مِنْ أَنْ يَأْكُلَ مِنْ عَمَلِ يَدَيْهِ قَالَ وَكَانَ دَاوُد لَا يَأْكُلُ إلاَّ مِنْ عَمَلِ يَدَيْهِ)).

وَبِه أَنبأَنَا الْبَيْهَقِيّ قَالَ أَنبأَنَا أَبو عَبْدُ اللهِ الْحَافِظُ قَالَ أخبرنِي جَعْفَر بن مُحَمَّد بن نصير قَالَ حَدثنِي الْجُنَيْد قَالَ سَمِعت السّري يَذُمُّ الْجُلُوس فِي الْمَسْجِد الْجَامِع وَيَقُول جعلُوا الْمَسْجِد الْجَامِع حوانيت لَيْسَ لَهَا أَبْوَاب.

وَبِهِ أَنبأَنَا الْبَيْهَقِيّ بِإِسْنَادِهِ عَن أَبِي بكر الصّديق رَضِي الله عَنهُ قَالَ دِيْنُكَ لِمَعَادِكَ وَدِرْهَمُكَ لِمَعَاشِكَ وَلَا خَيْر فِي امْرِئٍ بِلَا دِرْهَمٍ.

وَبِهِ أَنبأَنَا الْبَيْهَقِيّ قَالَ أَنبأَنَا أَبُو عبد الله الْحَافِظ قَالَ أخبرنِي جَعْفَر بن مُحَمَّد الْخَواص قَالَ أنبأنا إبراهيم بن نصر المنصوري قَالَ سَمِعت ابراهيم بن بشار خَادِم ابراهيم بن أدهم قَالَ سَمِعت أَبَا عَلِيّ الفضيل بن عِيَاض: يَقُول لِابْنِ الْمُبَارك أَنْت تَأْمُرنَا بالزُّهْدِ والتَّقَلُّلِ وَالْبُلغَةِ وَنَرَاكَ تَأْتِي بالبضائع من بِلَاد خُرَاسَانَ إِلَى الْبَلَد الْحَرَام؟ كَيفَ ذَا وَأَنت بِخِلَاف ذَا؟ فَقَالَ ابْن الْمُبَارك يَا أَبَا عَلِيّ! أَنا أفعلُ ذَا لِأَصُوْنَ بهَا وَجْهي وأُكْرِمَ بهَا عِرْضي. وأستعينَ بهَا على طَاعَةِ رَبِّي لَا أَرَى لله حَقًّا إِلَّا سَارَعْتُ اليه حَتَّى أقومَ بِهِ. فَقَالَ لَهُ الفضيل يَا ابْن الْمُبَارك مَا أحسن ذَا إِن تمّ ذَا.

13. Īmān that one must have tawakkul (rely) on Allāh Taʿālā

Allāh Taʿālā says: "And upon Allāh the believers should rely",[26] and: "Sufficient for us is Allāh, and (He is) the best Disposer of affairs.",[27] and: "And upon Allāh rely, if you should be believers",[28] and: "And whoever relies upon Allāh - then He is sufficient for him. Indeed, Allāh will accomplish His purpose; Allāh brings His command to pass." [29]

It is narrated in the Ṣaḥīḥayn by Ibn ʿAbbās ﵁, concerning his Ṣaḥaba's inquiry about the seventy thousand who would enter Jannah without reckoning, that the Prophet ﷺ said: "They are those who did not resort to cauterisation, or the use of (unlawful) charms, or divination, but relied on their Lord instead."

Reliance on Allāh is to hand one's affairs over to Him, and to have trust in Him, while taking into account the causality which He has preordained.

---

[26] Āl ʿImrān, 122.
[27] Āl ʿImrān, 173.
[28] Māida, 23.
[29] Talāq, 3.

It is narrated in Ṣaḥīḥ Bukhāri by al-Zubayr ﷺ that the Prophet ﷺ said “It is better that one of you should take a rope and go to the mountains, and return with a load of firewood on his back, which he then sells to become self-sufficient, instead of begging from others, who may give something to him, or may not.”

It is narrated in Ṣaḥīḥ Bukhāri by al-Miqdām ibn Maʿdikarib ﷺ that the Prophet ﷺ said: “The best food anyone can eat is that which is earnt by ones's own hands. Dawud عليه السلام used to only to eat from the money which he himself had earnt.”

Al-Junayd said that he heard al-Sari criticising the custom of sitting about in the Friday Masjid, saying: “They have turned the masjid into a market with no way out.”

Abū Bakr Siddīq ﷺ said “Your Dīn is for your future life, and your money is for your livelihood; there is no good in a man with no money to his name.”

Al-Fuḍayl ibn ʿIyāḍ once said to Ibn al-Mubārak, “You demand renunciation from us, yet you import merchandise from the land of Khurasān to Makkah. Why do you enjoin us to do something which you yourself avoid?” And he replied, “I do it to preserve my honour, and to assist myself in obeying my Lord.” And Fuḍayl said to him, “O Ibn al-Mubārak! That is a fine thing indeed, if it has such results!”

الرَّابِع عشر من شعب الإيمان

الإيمان بِوُجُوب محبَّة النَّبِي صلى الله عَلَيْهِ وَسلم لحَدِيث أنس رَضِي الله عَنهُ الْمُتَّفق على صِحَّته ((لَا يُؤمِنُ أَحَدُكُمْ حَتَّى أَكُوْنَ أَحَبَّ إِلَيْهِ مِنْ وَالِدِهِ وَوَلَدِهِ وَالنَّاسِ أجمعين)).

وَلِحَدِيث أنس رَضِي الله عَنهُ فِي الصَّحِيحَيْنِ ((ثَلَاثٌ مَنْ كُنَّ فِيهِ وَجَدَ بِهِنَّ حَلَاوَةَ الإِيمَانِ أَنْ يَكُوْنَ اللهُ وَرَسُولُهُ أَحَبَّ إِلَيْهِ مِمَّا سِوَاهُمَا)) الحَدِيث.

ولحديثه فيهمَا أيضا قَالَ ((جَاءَ رجل إِلَى النَّبِي صلى الله عَلَيْهِ وَسلم فَقَالَ يَا رَسُول

الله مَتى السَّاعَة؟ فَقَالَ مَا أَعدَدْت لَهَا؟ فَقَالَ يَا رَسُول الله مَا أعددت لَهَا كثير صِيَام وَلَا صَدَقَة إِلَّا أَنِّي أحب الله وَرَسُوله. قَالَ أنت مَعَ من أَحْبَبْت)).

14. Īmān in the obligation to love the Prophet ﷺ

It is narrated in the Ṣaḥīḥayn by Anas ﷺ that the Prophet ﷺ said, "None of you believes until I am dearer to him than his father, his child, and all mankind."
It is also narrated in the Ṣaḥīḥayn by Anas ﷺ that the Prophet ﷺ said, "There are three things which, when they are present in anyone, will cause him to taste the sweetness of Īmān: that Allāh and His Messenger be dearer to him than all else...".
It is also narrated in the Ṣaḥīḥayn that a man once came to the Prophet ﷺ and said, "O Messenger of Allāh! When will the Last Hour come?" The Messenger ﷺ asked "What have you set aside for it?" The man replied "O Messenger of Allāh! I have not set aside for it any great amount of fasting, or charity; and yet I love Allāh and His Messenger." And he told him, "You shall be with those whom you love."

الْخَامِس عشر من شعب الإيمان

الإيمان بِوُجُوب تَعْظِيم النَّبِي صلى الله عَلَيْهِ وَسلم وتجبيله وتوقيره لقَوْله تَعَالَى ﴿وَتُعَزِّرُوْهُ وَتُوَقِّرُوْهُ﴾ وَقَوله تَعَالَى ﴿فَالَّذِينَ آمَنُوا بِهِ وَعَزَّرُوْهُ وَنَصَرُوْهُ﴾ وَالتَّعْزِير هَا هُنَا التَّعْظِيم بِلَا خلاف وَقَوله تَعَالَى ﴿لَا تجْعَلُوْا دُعَآءَ الرَّسُولِ بَيْنَكُم كَدُعَآءِ بَعْضِكُمْ بَعْضًا﴾ أَي لَا تَقُوْلُوا لَهُ يَا مُحَمَّد! يَا أَبَا الْقَاسِم! بَلْ يَا رَسُولَ اللهِ يَا نَبِيَّ اللهِ وَلقَوْله تَعَالَى ﴿لَا تُقَدِّمُوْا بَيْنَ يَدَي اللهِ وَرَسُولِهِ﴾ وَقَوله تَعَالَى ﴿لَا تَرْفَعُوْا أَصْوَاتَكُمْ فَوق صَوْتَ النَّبِيِّ﴾ الأيَات.
وَبِه أنبأَنَا الْبَيْهَقِيّ قَالَ وَهَذِه منزلَة فَوق منزلَة الْمحبَّة إِذْ لَيْسَ كل مُحِبٍّ مُعَظِّمًا

كمحبة الأب لوَلَده وَالسَّيِّد لعَبْدِهِ من غير تَعْظِيم بِخِلَاف الْعَكْس.

15. Īmān in the obligation to honour, venerate and revere the Prophet ﷺ

Allāh Taʿālā says: "That you might honour and revere him",[30] and also: "So they who have believed in him, honored him, supported him",[31] and: "Do not make (your) calling of the Messenger among yourselves as the call of one of you to another",[32], i.e., address him as the 'Messenger of Allāh' or the 'Prophet of Allāh', rather than 'Muḥammed' or 'Abū Qāsim'. And He has said: "do not put (yourselves) before Allāh and His Messenger",[33] and: "Do not raise your voices above the voice of the Prophet." [34]
This is a higher degree than that of love, since not everyone who loves reveres: a father loves his child, and a master his slave, but does not revere him, whereas all who revere must love also.

السَّادِس عشر من شعب الإيمان

شح الْمَرْء بِدِينِهِ حَتَّى يكون الْقَذْف فِي النَّار أحب إِلَيْهِ من الْكفْر لحَدِيث أنس الْمُتَّفق عَلَيْهِ ((ثَلَاثٌ مَنْ كُنَّ فِيهِ وَجَدَ بِهِنَّ حَلَاوَةَ الإيمانِ، ثمَّ قَالَ وأن يُلْقَى فِي النَّار أَحَبُّ إليه مَنْ أنْ يَرْجِعَ إِلَى الْكفْرِ بَعْدَ أَنْ أَنْقَذَهُ اللهُ مِنْهُ)).
ولحديثه أَيْضًا فِي صَحِيح مُسلم أَنّ رَجُلًا سَأَلَ النَّبِيَّ صلى الله عَلَيْهِ وَسلم فَأَعْطَاهُ غَنَمًا بَين جَبَلَيْنِ فَأَتَى قَوْمَهُ فَقَالَ أَسْلَمُوا فوَاللّهِ إِنَّ مُحَمَّدًا ليعطي عَطاءَ رَجُلٍ لَا يَخَاف الْفَاقَةَ. فَقَالَ أنس وَإِن كَانَ الرجلُ يجِيءُ إِلَى النَّبِي صلى الله عَلَيْهِ وَسلم مَا

[30] Fatḥ, 9.
[31] Aʿrāf, 157.
[32] Nūr, 63.
[33] Hujurāt, 1.
[34] Hujurāt, 2.

يُرِيدُ إِلَّا الدُّنْيَا فَمَا يُمْسِي حَتَّى يكُونَ دينه أحبُّ إليه وأَعَزُّ مِنَ الدُّنْيَا بِمَا فِيهَا)).

16. One's firmness in his Dīn, so that he would rather be cast into the Fire than to leave Islam

It is narrated in the Ṣaḥīḥayn by Anas ﷺ that the Prophet ﷺ said, "There are three things which, when they are present in anyone, will cause him to taste the sweetness of faith: ... (one of which is) that he should loath to return to unbelief after Allāh had rescued him from it just as he would loath to be cast into a blazing fire".'
It is narrated in Ṣaḥīḥ Muslim by Anas ﷺ that the Prophet ﷺ said, "A man once begged from the Prophet ﷺ, and he gave him enough goats and sheep to fill a valley. He returned to his people, and said, 'Enter Islām! For, by Allāh, Muḥammed gives with no fear of poverty!' People would go to the Prophet ﷺ wanting only worldly goods, and would find before the day was out that their Dīn had become dearer and more precious to them than the whole world."

السَّابِع عشر من شعب الإيمان

طلب الْعلم وَهُوَ معرفَة الْبَارِي تَعَالَى وَمَا جَاءَ من عِنْد الله وَعلمُ النُّبُوَّة وَمَا يُمَيّز بِهِ النَّبِي صلى الله عَلَيْهِ وَسلم عَن غَيره وَعلمُ أَحكام الله تَعَالَى وأَقْضِيَتِهِ وَمَعْرِفَةُ مَا تطلب الأَحكام مِنْهُ كالكتاب وَالسّنةِ وَالْقِيَاس وشروط الإِجْتِهَاد.

وَالْقرَانُ والحَدِيثُ مشحونان بفضيلةِ الْعلمِ وَالْعُلَمَاءِ. قَالَ الله تَعَالَى ﴿إِنَّمَا يَخْشَى اللهَ مِنْ عِبَادِهِ الْعُلَمَاءُ﴾ وَقَالَ تَعَالَى ﴿شَهِدَ اللهُ أَنَّهُ لَا إِلَهَ إِلَّا هُوَ وَالْمَلَائِكَةُ وَأُولُوا الْعِلْمِ قَائِمًا بِالْقِسْطِ﴾ وَقَالَ تَعَالَى ﴿وَعَلَّمَكَ مَا لَمْ تَكُنْ تَعْلَمُ وَكَانَ فَضْلُ اللهِ عَلَيْكَ عَظِيمًا﴾ وَقَالَ تَعَالَى ﴿يَرْفَعُ اللهُ الَّذِيْنَ آمَنُوْا مِنْكُمْ وَالَّذِيْنَ أُوْتُوا الْعِلْمَ دَرَجَاتٍ﴾ وَقَالَ تَعَالَى ﴿هَلْ يَسْتَوِي الَّذين يَعْلَمُوْنَ وَالَّذين لَا يَعْلَمُوْنَ إِنَّمَا

يتَذَكَّر أوْلُوا الأَلْبَابِ﴾.

وَفِي الصَّحِيحَيْنِ من حَدِيث عبد الله بن عَمْرو بن الْعَاصِ رَضِي الله عَنْهُمَا ((إِن اللهَ لَا يَقْبِضُ الْعِلْمَ إِنْتِزَاعًا. يَنْتَزِعُهُ مِنَ النَّاسِ وَلَكِنْ يَقْبِضُ الْعِلْمَ بِقَبضِ الْعُلَمَاءِ حَتَّى إِذَا لَمْ يُبْقِ عَالِمًا إِتَّخَذَ النَّاسُ رُؤُوْسًا جُهَّالًا فَسُئِلُوْا فَأَفْتَوْا بِغَيْرِ عِلْمٍ فَضَلُّوْا وَأَضَلُّوْا)).

وَفِي صَحِيح مُسلم من حَدِيث أبي هُرَيْرَة رَضِي الله عَنهُ ((مَنْ نَفَّسَ عَنْ مُؤْمِنٍ كُرْبَةً مِنْ كُرَبِ الدُّنْيَا نَفَّسَ اللهُ عَنْهُ كُرْبَةً مِنْ كُرَبِ يَوْمَ الْقِيَامَةِ، وَمَنْ يَسَّرَ عَلَى مُعْسِرٍ يَسَّرَ اللهُ عَلَيْهِ فِي الدُّنْيَا والْآخِرَةِ، وَمَنْ سَتَرَ مُسْلِمًا سَتَرَهُ اللهُ فِي الدُّنْيَا والآخِرَةِ، وَاللهُ فِي عَوْنِ العَبْدِ مَا كَانَ العَبْدُ فِي عَوْنِ أَخِيْهِ، وَمَنْ سَلَكَ طَرِيْقًا يَلْتَمِسُ فِيْهِ عِلْمًا سَهَّلَ اللهُ لَهُ بِهِ طَرِيْقًا إِلَى الْجَنَّةِ، وَمَا إِجْتَمَعَ قَوْمٌ فِيْ بَيْتٍ مِنْ بُيُوْتِ اللهِ يَتْلُوْنَ كِتَابَ اللهِ وَيَتَدَارَسُونَهُ بَيْنَهُمْ إِلَّا نَزَلَتْ عَلَيْهِمْ السَّكِينَةُ وَحَفَّتْهُمْ الْمَلَائِكَةُ وَغَشِيَتْهُمْ الرَّحْمَةُ وَذَكَرَهُمْ اللهُ فِيمَنْ عِنْدَهُ، وَمَنْ بَطَّأَ بِهِ عَمَلُهُ لَمْ يُسْرِعْ بِهِ نَسَبُهُ)).

17. Seeking ʿilm (knowledge)

Seeking ʿilm of the Exalted Creator, and that which has come from Him, and ʿilm that prophets have been sent with, and ʿilm of their distinguishing attributes, and of the Laws of Allāh Taʿālā, and of the sources which His Laws are to be sought from, such as the Book, the Sunna, Qiyās (analogy) and ijtihād (the conditions for independent scholarly judgement).

The Qurʾān and Ḥadīth are full of statements about the merit of ʿilm and the ʿulamā. Allāh Taʿālā says: "Only those fear Allāh, from among His servants, who have knowledge",[35] and: "Allāh witnesses that there is no deity except Him, and (so do) the angels and those

[35] Nūr, 28.

of knowledge – (that He is) maintaining (creation) in justice",[36] and "He has taught you that which you did not know. And ever has the favor of Allāh upon you been great",[37] and: "Allāh will raise those who have believed among you and those who were given knowledge, by degrees", [38] and "Are those who know equal to those who do not know? Only they will remember (who are) people of understanding."[39]

It is narrated in the Ṣaḥīḥayn by Ibn ʿAmr ﷺ that the Prophet ﷺ said, "Allāh does not remove ʿilm by snatching it away from mankind; but does so rather by bringing to an end the lives of those who possess it, until there shall come a time when not a single learned man remains, and people appoint ignorant leaders for themselves, who when asked give opinions while having no ʿilm. Being themselves astray, they cause others to stray also."

It is narrated in Ṣaḥīḥ Muslim by Abū Hurayra ﷺ that the Prophet ﷺ said, "Whoever rescues a believer from a worldly calamity shall have Allāh rescue him from one of the calamities of the Day of Reserruction. Whoever is kind to a bankrupt, to him Allāh shall be kind in this world and in the next. Whoever conceals the fault of a Muslim, for him Allāh shall conceal his faults in this world and in the next. Allāh helps His slave as long as His slave helps his brother. Whoever treads a path in order to seek ʿilm, for him Allāh shall make easy a path to Jannah. Never did a group of people gather in one of the houses of Allāh in order to recite His book, and study it amongst themselves, except that Allāh's tranquillity will descend upon them, the Angels throng around them, and mercy cover them, and Allāh makes mention of them in His presence. When a man falls behind due to his actions, his lineage will not hasten him forward."

---

[36] Āl ʿImrān, 18.

[37] Nisā, 113.

[38] Mujadila, 11

[39] Zumar, 9.

الثَّامِن عشر من شعب الإيمان

نَشْر الْعلم لقَوْله تَعَالَى ﴿لِتُبَيِّنُنَّهُ لِلنَّاسِ وَلَا تَكْتُمُوْنَهُ﴾ وَقوله تَعَالَى ﴿وَلِيُنْذِرُوْا قَوْمَهُمْ إِذا رَجَعُوْا إِلَيْهِمْ﴾.

وَلِحَدِيث أبي بكرَة رَضِي الله عَنهُ فِي الصَّحِيحَيْنِ أن النَّبِي صلى الله عَلَيْهِ وَسلم قَالَ فِي خطبَته بمنى ((أَلَا لِيُبَلِّغَنَّ الشَّاهِدُ مِنْكُمْ الْغَائِبَ فَلَعَلَّ مَنْ يُبَلِّغُهُ يَكُوْنُ أَوْعَى لَهُ مِنْ بَعْضِ مَنْ سَمِعَهُ)).

وَحَدِيث أبي هُرَيْرَة فِي سنَن أبي دَاوُد ((مَنْ سُئِلَ عَنْ عِلْمٍ فَكَتَمَهُ أَلْجَمَهُ اللهُ بِلِجَامٍ مِنَ النَّارِ يَوْمَ الْقِيَامَةِ)).

وروى الْبَيْهَقِيّ بِإِسْنَادِهِ عَن الإمامِ عُمَرَ بن عَبْدِ الْعَزِيزِ الأُمَوِيِّ رَحْمَةُ اللهِ عَلَيْهِ أَنَّهُ قَالَ مَنْ لم يَعُدَّ كَلَامه من عمله كثرت خطاياه وَمن عمل بِغَيْر علم كَانَ مَا يفْسد أكثر مِمَّا يصلح.

وَعَن الْحَارِث المحاسبي الْعلم يُورِثُ الخشيةَ والزُّهْدُ يُورِثُ الرَّاحَةَ والمعرفة تُوْرِثُ الإنَابَةَ. وَعَن إبْن سعد أَن من عَمِلَ بِعِلْمِ الرِّوَايَةِ وَرِثَ علم الدِّرَايَة وَمن عمل بِعلْمِ الدِّرَايَة ورث علم الرِّعَايَة وَمن عمل بِعلم الرِّعَايَة هُدِيَ إِلى سَبِيل الْحق. وَعَن مَالِك بن دِينَار إِذا طلب العَبْدُ الْعلمَ لِيَعْمَلَ بِهِ كَسره علمه وَإِذا طلبه لغير الْعَمَل زَاده كبرًا.

وَعَن مَعْرُوف الْكَرْخِي إِذا أَرَادَ الله بِعَبْدٍ خيرا فَتَحَ عَلَيْهِ بَاب الْعَمَل وأغلق عَلَيْهِ بَاب الجَدَلِ وَإِذا أَرَادَ الله بِعَبْدٍ شرا أغلق عَلَيْهِ بَاب الْعَمَلِ وَفتح عَلَيْهِ بَاب الجَدَلِ.

وَعَن أبي بكر الْورّاق من أكْتفى بالْكَلَام من الْعلم دون الزُّهْدِ وَالْفِقْه تزندق، وَمن إكْتفى بالزهد دون الْفِقْه وَالْكَلَام إبتدع، وَمن إكْتفى بالفقه دون الزّهْد

والورع تفسق، وَمن تفنن فِي الأمور كلهَا تخلص.
وَعَن الْحسن الْبَصْرِيّ رَحمَه الله أنه مر عَلَيْهِ رجل فَقيل هَذَا فَقيه فَقَالَ أَو تَدْرُونَ من الْفَقِيه إِنَّمَا الْفَقِيه الْعَالم فِي دينه الزَّاهِد فِي دُنْيَاهُ الْقَائِم على عبَادَة ربه.
وَعَن مَالك بن دِينَار قَالَ قَرَأت فِي التوارة إِن الْعَالم إِذا لم يعْمل بِعِلْمِهِ زلت موعظته من الْقُلُوب كَمَا يزل الْقَطْرُ عَن الصَّفَا. وأنشد عَن أبي بكر بن أبي دَاوُد لِنَفسِهِ:

مَنْ غَصَّ دَاوَى بِشُرْبِ الْمَاءِ غُصَّتَهُ ... فَكَيْفَ يَصْنَعُ مَنْ قَدْ غَصَّ بِالْمَاءِ.
وَعَن أبي عُثْمَان الْحِيرِي الزَّاهِد:

وَغيرُ تَقِيٍّ يَأْمُرُ النَّاسَ بِالتَّقَى ... طَبِيبٌ يُدَاوِي والطبيبُ مَرِيضُ
نسْأَلُ الله التَّوْفِيق للْعلم وَالْعَمَل ونعوذ بِجلَال وَجهه من الْخذلَان والحرص والأمل.

18. Spreading Knowledge

Allāh Taʿālā says: "You must make it clear to the people and not conceal it!",[40] and: "For there should separate from every division of them a group (remaining) to obtain understanding in the Dīn and warn their people when they return to them that they might be cautious."[41]

It is narrated in the Ṣaḥīḥayn by Abū Bakra ؓ that the Prophet ﷺ said in his Sermon at Minā, "Let those who are present inform those who are not. And it may be that those who pass it on understand it less than some of those who hear it."

It is narrated in Abū Dāwūd by Abū Hurayra ؓ that the Prophet ﷺ said, "Whoever is asked about something he knows, and conceals it, shall be made by Allāh to wear a bridle of fire on the Day of

---

[40] Āl ʿImrān, 187.
[41] Tawba, 122.

Reserruction."

The Khalīfa ʿUmar ibn ʿAbdul ʿAzīz said, "Whoever does not consider his speech to be part of his actions will sin abundantly, and whoever acts without ʿilm will do more harm than good."

Al-Muḥāsibi said: "Knowledge (of Dīn) begets the fear of Allāh, renunciation begets calm, and ʿilm (of Allāh) begets repentance."

According to Ibn Saʿd, "Whoever acts according to ʿilm from the āḥadīth, will be given ʿilm from insight, and whoever acts according to ʿilm from insight, will be given the ʿilm of obedience, and whoever acts according to the ʿilm of obedience will be guided to Allāh's path."

Mālik ibn Dīnār said, "When one of Allāh's slaves seeks ʿilm in order to act in accordance therewith, his ʿilm makes him modest. But when he seeks it for any other reason, he becomes arrogant."

Maʿrūf al-Karkhi said, "Whenever Allāh wishes to do good to His slave, He opens the door of action for him, and closes the door of argument. But when He wishes evil for His slave, He closes the door of action for him, and opens the door of argument."

Abū Bakr al-Warrāq said, "Whoever suffices himself with kalām (theology) without being a man of renunciation and Fiqh, becomes a heretic. Whoever suffices himself with renunciation without the Fiqh and kalaam, commits a harmful innovation. Whoever suffices himself with Fiqh without renunciation and scrupulousness becomes corrupt. But whoever does all of these things will be saved."

Ḥasan Baṣri said, "A man once passed me, and I was told that he was a scholar of Fiqh. 'Do you know what a true scholar of Fiqh is?' I asked. 'A true scholar of Fiqh is a man who is learned about his Dīn, renounces the things of this world, and who spends much time in the worship of his Lord'."

Mālik ibn Dīnār said that "I have read in the Tawrāt that the sermons of a learned man who does not act by his ʿilm will have no effect on people's hearts, as though they were raindrops falling on a stone."

Ibn Abī Dāwūd composed the following couplet:

A man who chokes may find relief in drinking;
But what shall he do whom the water chokes?

And the ascetic Abū ʿUthmān al-Ḥīri said:

An impious man enjoining others to piety
Is like a sick doctor who tries to cure others.

We pray to Allāh to grant us success in learning and acting; we seek the protection of His majestic countenance from failure, greed, and vain hopes!

التَّاسِع عشر من شعب الإيمان

تَعْظِيم الْقرَان الْمجِيد بتعلمه وتعليمه وَحفظ حُدُوده وأحكامه وَعلم حَلَاله وَحَرَامه وتبجيل أهله وحفاظه وإستشعارها يهيج إلى الْبكاء من مواعيد الله عز وَجل ووعيده.

قَالَ الله تَعَالَى ﴿لَوْ أَنْزَلْنَا هَذَا الْقُرْآنَ عَلَى جَبَلٍ لَرَأَيْتَهُ خَاشِعًا مُتَصَدِّعًا مِنْ خَشْيَةِ اللَّه﴾

وَقَالَ تَعَالَى ﴿إِنَّهُ لَقُرْآنٌ كَرِيْمٌ فِيْ كِتَابٍ مَكْنُونٍ لَا يَمَسُّهُ إِلَّا الْمُطَّهُرُوْنَ تَنْزِيْلٌ مِن رَبِّ الْعَالَمِيْنَ﴾ وَقَالَ تَعَالَى ﴿وَلَوْ أَنَّ قُرْآنًا سُيِّرَتْ بِهِ الْجِبَالُ أَوْ قُطِّعَتْ بِهِ الْأَرْضُ أَوْ كُلِّمَ بِهِ الْمَوْتَى بَل لِلَّهِ الْأَمْرُ جَمِيْعًا﴾.

قَالَ النَّبِي صلى الله عَلَيْهِ وَسلم رَوَاهُ الْبُخَارِيّ عَن عُثْمَان بن عَفَّان رَضِي الله عَنهُ ((أَفْضَلُكُمْ أَوْ خَيْرُكُمْ مَنْ تَعَلَّمَ الْقُرْآنَ وَعَلَّمَهُ)).

وَقَالَ فِيمَا رَوَاهُ الْبُخَارِيّ وَمُسلم فِي صَحِيحَيْهِمَا عَنْ أَبِيْ مُوْسَى الأَشعري رَضِي الله عَنهُ ((تَعَاهَدُوا الْقرَانَ فَوَالَّذِيْ نَفْسُ مُحَمَّدٍ بِيَدِهِ لَهُوَ أَشَدُّ تَفَلُّتًا مِنَ الإِبِلِ فِي عُقُلِهَا)).

وَقَالَ فِيمَا رَوَيَاهُ عَنْ عَبْدِ اللهِ بنِ عُمَرَ رَضِي الله عَنهُمَا ((لَا حَسَدَ إِلَّا فِي اثْنَتَيْنِ رَجُلٌ آتَاهُ اللهُ هَذَا الْكِتَابَ فَقَامَ بِهِ آنَاء اللَّيْل وَالنَّهَار وَرجل آتَاهُ الله مَالًا فَهُوَ يَتَصَدَّقُ بِهِ آنَاءَ اللَّيْلِ وَالنَّهَارِ)) وَقَالَ فِيمَا رَوَاهُ مُسلِم عَن عُمَرَ رَضِي الله عَنهُ

((إِنَّ اللهَ يَرْفَعُ بِهَذَا الْكِتَابِ أَقْوَامًا وَيَضَعُ بِهِ آخَرِيْنَ)).

19. The Veneration of the Qur'ān Majīd

This is accomplished by learning and teaching it, and memorising and respecting its laws and provisions, and knowing thereby what is permissible and what is forbidden, and also by honouring those who understand and have memorised it, and by making oneself aware of Allāh's promises and threats which inspire weeping.

Allāh Ta'ālā says: "If We had sent down this Qur'ān upon a mountain, you would have seen it humbled and coming apart from fear of Allāh",[42] and: "In a Register well-protected; None touch it except the purified. (It is) a revelation from the Lord of the worlds.",[43] and "And if there was any Qur'ān by which the mountains would be removed or the earth would be broken apart or the dead would be made to speak, (it would be this Qur'ān), but to Allāh belongs the affair entirely."[44]

It is narrated in the Ṣaḥīḥayn by 'Uthmān bin 'Affān ﷺ that the Prophet ﷺ said, "The best of you is he who learns and teaches the Qur'ān."

It is also narrated in the Ṣaḥīḥayn by Abū Mūsa al-Ash'ari ﷺ that the Prophet ﷺ said, "Hold fast constantly to this Qur'ān, for by Him in Whose hand lies the soul of Muḥammed, it escapes more easily than does a camel from its rope."

It is also narrated in the Ṣaḥīḥayn by Ibn 'Umar ﷺ that the Prophet ﷺ said, "Envy is permissible only in respect of two men: one whom Allāh gives this book, and who stands reciting it day and night, and a man whom Allāh gives wealth, which he gives in charity day and night."

It is also narrated in Ṣaḥīḥ Muslim by 'Umar ﷺ that the Prophet ﷺ said, "Indeed, Allāh elavates through this book some people, and degrades others."

---

42 Ḥashr, 21.

43 Wāqi'a, 77-80.

44 Ar-Ra'd, 31.

الْعِشْرُونَ من شعب الإيمان

الطهارات لقَوْله تَعَالَى ﴿إِذا قُمْتُم إِلَى الصَّلَاةِ فَاغْسِلُوا وُجُوهَكُم وَأَيْدِيَكُمْ إِلَى الْمَرَافِقِ﴾.

وَلِحَدِيث أبي مَالك الأشعري رَضِي الله عَنهُ فِي صَحِيح مُسلم ((الطُّهُوْرُ شَطْرُ الْإِيْمَانِ، وَالْحَمْد لله تَمْلَأُ الْمِيْزَانِ، وَسُبْحَانَ اللهِ وَاللهُ أَكْبَرُ تَمْلَآنِ اَوْ تَمْلَأُ مَا بَيْنَ السَّمَاءِ وَالْأَرْضِ، وَالصَّلَاةُ نُوْرٌ، وَالصَّدَقَةُ بُرْهَانٌ، وَالصَّبْرُ ضِيَاءٌ، وَالْقُرْآنُ حُجَّةٌ لَكَ أَوْ عَلَيْكَ. كُلُّ النَّاسِ يَغْدُوْ فَبَائِعٌ نَفْسَهُ فَمُعْتِقُهَا أَوْ مُوْبِقُهَا)).

وَلِحَدِيثِ إِبْنِ عُمَرَ رَضِي اللهُ عَنْهُمَا فِي صَحِيح مُسلم أيضًا ((لَا يَقبَلُ اللهُ عز وَجل صَلَاةً بِغَيْرِ طُهُورٍ وَلَا صَدَقَةٍ مِنْ غُلُولٍ)).

وَلِحَدِيث حسن عَن أبي كَبْشَة السَّلُولِي عَن ثَوْبَان رَضِي الله عَنهُ ((اسْتَقِيمُوا وَلنْ تُحْصُوا وَاعْلَمُوا أَنَّ خَيْرَ أَعْمَالِكُمْ الصَّلَاةُ وَلَا يُحَافِظُ عَلَى الْوضُوءِ إِلَّا مُؤْمِنٌ)).

روى الْحَلِيمِيّ عَن يحي بن آدم فِي قَوْله صلى الله عَلَيْهِ وَسلم ((الطُّهُوْرُ شَطْرُ الإِيْمَانِ لِأَنَّ اللهَ تَعَالَى سَمَّى الصَّلَاةَ إِيمَانًا فَقَالَ ﴿وَمَا كَانَ اللهُ لِيُضِيعَ إِيمَانَكُمْ﴾ أَي صَلَاتَكُمْ إِلى بَيت الْمُقدس وَلَا تجوز الصَّلَاةُ إِلَّا بِالْوضُوءِ فهما شَيْئَانِ كل وَاحِد مِنْهُمَا نصف اللآخر)).

20. Purification

Allāh Taʿālā says: "When you rise to (perform) ṣalāt, wash your faces and your forearms to the elbows and wipe over your heads and wash your feet to the ankles."[45]

It is narrated in Ṣaḥīḥ Muslim by Abū Mālik al-Ashʿari ﵁ that the Prophet ﷺ said "Purification is half of Īmān, '*Alḥamdulillah* - Praise be to Allāh!' fills the Scale, '*SubhānAllāh* – Glory to Allāh' and '*Allāhu*

[45] Māida, 6.

Akbar –Allāh is the greatest' fills all that is between heaven and earth. Salāt is a light, charity is a proof, steadfastness is radiance, and the Qur'ān is an argument for you or against you. All people shall come, some having sold their souls, either freeing them or bringing about their destruction."

It is narrated in Ṣaḥīḥ Muslim by Ibn 'Umar ﷺ that the Prophet ﷺ said, "Allāh ﷻ, does not accept salāt without tahārat and no charity (is accepted) that comes from fraud."

It is narrated (in Musnad Aḥmad & Sunan Ibn Māja) by Thawbān ﷺ reported that the Prophet ﷺ said: "Live uprightly, for you will not do everything; and know that the finest of all your acts is ṣalāt. Only a believer maintains his wuḍu."

According to al-Ḥalmī, Yaḥyā ibn Ādam remarked regarding the ḥadīth "Purification is half of Īmān", because Allāh Ta'ālā has referred to ṣalāt as Īmān, saying, "And never would Allāh have caused you to lose your Īmān",[46] meaning your ṣalāt towards Jerusalem, and ṣalāt is permissible only when one has wuḍu. They are two things (ṣalāt and wuḍu are two separate distinct acts). Each is a half of the other."

الْحَادِي وَالْعِشْرُونَ من شعب الإيمان

الصَّلَوَات الْخمس لقَوْله تَعَالَى ﴿وَمَا كَانَ اللهُ لِيُضِيعَ إِيْمَانَكُمْ﴾ أَي صَلَاتَكُمْ وَقوله تَعَالَى ﴿وَأَقِيمُوا الصَّلَاةَ وَآتُوا الزَّكَاةَ﴾ وَقوله تَعَالَى ﴿إِنَّ الصَّلَوةَ كَانَتْ عَلَى الْمُؤمِنِينَ كِتَابًا مَوْقُوْتًا﴾.

وَلِحَدِيث جَابر رَضِي الله عَنهُ فِي صَحِيح مُسلم ((إِنَّ بَيْنَ الرَّجُلِ وَبَيْنَ الشِرْكِ وَالْكُفْرِ تَرْكَ الصَّلَاةِ)).

وَحَدِيث عبد الله بن مَسْعُود رَضِي الله عَنهُ فِي الصَّحِيحَيْنِ قَالَ سَأَلتُ النَّبِيَّ صلى الله عَلَيْهِ وَسلم أَي الأعمال أحب إلى الله عز وَجل؟ قَالَ ((الصَّلَاةُ لِوَقْتهَا)). قلت

[46] Baqarah, 143.

ثمَّ أَيّ؟ قَالَ ((بِرُّ الْوَالِدَيْنِ)). قُلْتُ ثم أَيّ؟ قَالَ ((الْجِهَادُ فِي سَبِيلِ الله)). قَالَ وحَدثني بِهِنَّ وَلَوْ استزدتُه لَزادَنِي.

وَحَدِيث ابْن عمر رَضِي الله عَنْهُمَا فيهمَا ((صَلَاةُ الْجَمَاعَة أفضلُ من صَلَاةِ الْفَذِّ بِسَبْعٍ وَعشرِيْنَ دَرَجَةً)).

وَحَدِيث عُثْمَان رَضِي الله عَنهُ فِي صَحِيح مُسلم ((مَا مِنْ إمْرِىءٍ مُسْلِمٍ تَحْضُرُهُ صَلَاةٌ مَكْتُوبَةٌ فَيُحْسِنُ وُضُوءَهَا، وَخُشُوعَهَا، وَرُكُوعَهَا إلا كَانَت كَفَّارَةً لِمَا قَبْلَهَا مِنَ الذُّنُوبِ، مَا لَمْ يَأْتِ كَبِيرَةً وَذَلِكَ الدَّهْرَ كُلَّهُ)).

وَبِه أنبأَنَا الْبَيْهَقِيّ قَالَ وَلَيْسَ فِي الْعِبَادَات بعد الإيمان بِالله الرافعِ للكفر عبَادَةٌ سَمَّاهَا جلّ وَعلا إيمانا، وسمَّى رَسُولُ الله صلى الله عَلَيْهِ وَسلم تَركهَا كفرًا، إلا الصَّلَاة.

21. The Five ṣalāts

Allāh Taʿālā says: "And never would Allāh have caused you to lose your Īmān",[47] meaning "your ṣalāt": and also: "Establish ṣalāt, and give the zakāt",[48] and: "Indeed, ṣalāt has been decreed upon the believers a decree of specified times."[49]

It is narrated in Ṣaḥīḥ Muslim by Jābir ﵁ that the Prophet ﷺ said that "That which separates a person from polytheism and unbelief is ṣalāt."

It is narrated in the Ṣaḥīḥayn that Ibn Masʿūd ﵁ said that "I once asked the Prophet ﷺ which action was most beloved to Allāh, and he replied, 'The ṣalāt at its correct time.' I asked what came next, and he said. 'Kindness to parents.' I asked him what came after that, and he answered, 'Jihād in the path of Allāh'."

It is narrated in the Ṣaḥīḥayn by Ibn ʿUmar ﵄ that the Prophet ﷺ

---

[47] Baqarah, 143.

[48] Baqarah, 43.

[49] Nisā, 103.

said, “The ṣalāt is twenty-seven times more virtuous when said with a jamāʿa."
It is narrated in Ṣaḥīḥ Muslim by ʿUthmān ﵁ that the Prophet ﷺ said that “Whenever an obligatory ṣalāt-time comes to any Muslim, and he carries out his wuḍu, his humility and his rukuʿ properly, these things atone for all his previous sins (with the exception of major ones), and this holds true for all time.”
In this regard al-Bayhaqī commented, “After faith in Allāh, which releases one from kufr, there is no act of worship finer and more exalted than ṣalāt, the abandonment of which Allāh's Messenger ﷺ termed kufr itself.”

الثَّانِي وَالْعِشْرُونَ من شعب الإيمان

الزَّكَاة لقَوْله تَعَالَى ﴿وَمَا أُمِرُوْا إِلاَّ لِيَعْبُدُوْا اللهَ مُخْلِصِيْنَ لَهُ الدِّيْنَ حُنَفَاءَ وَيُقِيْمُوْا الصَّلَاةَ وَيُؤْتُوا الزَّكَاةَ وَذٰلِكَ دِيْنُ الْقَيِّمَةِ﴾وَقوله تعَالَى ﴿وَالَّذين يَكْنِزُوْنَ الذَّهَبَ وَالْفِضَّةَ وَلَا يُنْفِقُونَهَا فِي سَبِيْلِ اللهِ فَبَشِّرْهُمْ بِعَذَابٍ أَلِيْمٍ يَوْمَ يُحْمَى عَلَيْهَا فِي نَارِ جَهَنَّمَ فَتُكْوَى بهَا جِباهُهُم وَجُنُوْبُهُمْ وَظُهُوْرُهُمْ هٰذَا مَا كَنَزْتُمْ لِأَنْفُسِكُمْ فَذُوقُوا مَا كُنْتُم تَكْنِزُوْنَ﴾ وَقوله تعَالَى ﴿وَلَا يَحْسَبَنَّ الَّذِيْنَ يَبْخَلُون بِمَا آتَاهُمُ اللهُ مِنْ فَضْلِهِ هُوَ خَيْرًا لَهُمْ بَلْ هُوَ شَرٌّ لَهُمْ سَيُطَوَّقُوْنَ مَا بَخِلُوْا بِهِ يَوْمَ الْقِيَامَةِ﴾.

وَلِحَدِيث إِبْن عَبَّاسٍ رَضِي الله عَنْهُمَا فِي الصَّحِيحَيْنِ أن رَسُول الله صلى الله عَلَيْهِ وَسلم لما بعث معَاذًا إِلى الْيمن قَالَ لَه ((إِنَّكَ تَأْتِيْ قَوْمًا أَهْلَ كِتَابٍ فَادْعُهُمْ إلى شَهَادَة أَن لَا إِلٰه الا الله وَأَنِّي رَسُول الله. فَإِنْ هُمْ أجابوك لِذَلِك، فَأَعْلِمْهُمْ أَنَّ اللهَ قَدْ افْتَرَضَ عَلَيْهِم خَمْسَ صَلَوَاتٍ فِي كُلِّ يَوْمٍ وَلَيْلَةٍ. فَإِنْ هُمْ أجابوك لِذَلِك، فَأَعْلِمْهُمْ أَنَّ اللهَ قَدْ افْتَرَضَ عَلَيْهِم صَدَقَةً فِي أَمْوَالِهِمْ تُؤْخَذُ مِنْ أَغْنِيَائِهِمْ وَتُرَدُّ عَلَى فُقَرَائِهِمْ. فَإِنْ هُمْ أَجَابُوْكَ لِذَلِكَ، فإِيَّاكَ وَكَرَائِمَ أَمْوَالِهِمْ، وَإِيَّاكَ وَدَعْوَةَ الْمَظْلُومِ

فَإِنَّهُ لَيْسَ بَيْنَهَا وَبَيْنَ اللهِ حِجَابٌ)).

وَحَدِيث أَبِي هُرَيْرَة فِي صَحِيح الْبُخَارِيّ ((مَنْ آتَاهُ اللهُ مَالًا فَلَمْ يُؤَدِّ زَكَاتَهُ مُثِّلَ لَهُ مَالُهُ يَوْمَ الْقِيَامَةِ شُجَاعًا أَقْرَعَ لَهُ زَبِيبَتَانِ يُطَوَّقُهُ ثُمَّ يَأْخُذُ بِلِهْزِمَتَيْهِ يَعْنِي شِدْقَيْهِ ثُمَّ يَقُول أنا مَالُكَ أنا كَنْزُكَ ثمَّ تَلا هَذِهِ الآيَة ﴿وَلَا يَحْسَبَنَّ الَّذِيْنَ يَبْخَلُونَ بِمَا آتَاهُمُ اللهُ مِنْ فَضْلِهِ هُوَ خَيْرًا لَهُمْ بَلْ هُوَ شَرٌّ لَهُمْ سَيُطَوَّقُوْنَ مَا بَخِلُوْا بِهِ يَوْمَ الْقِيَامَةِ﴾.

22. The Zakāt

Allāh Taʿālā says: "And they were not commanded except to worship Allāh, (being) sincere to Him in Dīn, inclining to truth, and to establish ṣalāt and to give zakāt. And that is the correct Dīn",[50] and: ""And those who hoard gold and silver and spend it not in the way of Allāh - give them tidings of a painful punishment, The Day when it will be heated in the fire of Hell and seared therewith will be their foreheads, their flanks, and their backs, (it will be said), "This is what you hoarded for yourselves, so taste what you used to hoard",'[51] "And let not those who (greedily) withhold what Allāh has given them of His bounty ever think that it is better for them. Rather, it is worse for them. Their necks will be encircled by what they withheld on the Day of Resurrection". [52]

It is narrated in the Ṣaḥīḥayn that Ibn ʿAbbās ﷺ that when Prophet ﷺ sent Muʿādh ﷺ to Yemen, he told him, "You are going to a people who have a Scripture, so call them to testify that there is none worthy of worship except Allāh, and that I am Rasulullāh. If they accept this, then teach them that Allāh has obligated five ṣalāts upon them every day. If they accept this, then teach them that Allāh has obligated upon them a charity to be taken from the wealthy among them and given to their poor. If they accept this,

---

[50] Bayyinah, 5.

[51] Tawba, 34-35.

[52] Āl ʿImrān, 180.

then beware of taking any more of their wealth! Beware also of the du'ā of the oppressed, for there is no veil between such a du'ā and Allāh."

It is narrated in Ṣaḥīḥ Bukhari by Abū Hurayra ﷺ that the Prophet ﷺ said that "Whoever is given wealth by Allāh and does not pay the zakāt due thereupon shall find that on the Day of Reserruction it is made to appear to him as a hairless snake with two black specks, which chains him, and then seizes him by his jaw and says, 'I am your wealth! I am your treasure!'" Then he recited the verse, "And let not those who (greedily) withhold what Allāh has given them of His bounty ever think that it is better for them. Rather, it is worse for them. Their necks will be encircled by what they withheld on the Day of Resurrection."

الثَّالِث وَالْعشْرُونَ من شعب الإيمان

الصّيام لقَوْله تَعَالَى ﴿كُتِبَ عَلَيْكُمُ الصِّيَامُ كَمَا كُتِبَ عَلَى الَّذِيْنَ مِنْ قَبْلِكُمْ﴾.
وَالحَدِيث عبد الله بن عمر رَضِي الله عَنْهُمَا فِي الصَّحِيحَيْنِ ((بُنِيَ الإسلامُ عَلَى خَمْسٍ شَهَادَةِ أَن لَا إِلٰه الا الله وَأَنَّ مُحَمَّدًا عَبْدُهُ وَرَسُوْلُهُ وإقامِ الصَّلَاةِ وإيْتاءِ الزَّكَاةِ وَصَوْمِ رَمَضَانَ وَحَجِّ الْبَيْتِ)).
وَحَدِيث أبي هُرَيْرَة رَضِي الله عَنهُ فيهمَا ((كُلُّ عَمَلِ ابْنِ آدَمَ يُضَاعَفُ، الحَسَنَةُ بِعَشْرِ أَمْثَالِهَا إِلَى سَبْعِمِائَةَ ضِعْفٍ. قَالَ الله عز وَجل إلاَّ الصَّوْمَ فَإِنَّهُ لِيْ وَأَنَا أَجْزِيْ بِهِ، يَدَعُ طَعَامَهُ وَشَهْوَتَهُ مِنْ أَجَلِيْ. للصَّائِمِ فَرْحَتَانِ: فَرْحَةٌ عِنْد فِطْرِهِ وَفَرْحَةٌ عِنْدَ لِقَاءِ رَبِّهِ. وَلَخُلُوْفُ فَمِ الصَّائِمِ أَطْيَبُ عِنْدَ اللهِ مِنْ رِيْحِ الْمِسْكِ. الصَّوْمُ جُنَّةٌ)).

23. Fasting

Allāh Ta'ālā says: "Decreed upon you is fasting as it was decreed upon those before you".[53]

[53] Baqarah, 183.

It is narrated in the Ṣaḥīḥayn by Ibn ʿUmar ؓ that the Prophet ﷺ said that "Islam is built on five things: Testimony that there is none worthy of worship except Allāh and that Muḥammed is the slave and messenger of Allāh, the establishment of ṣalāt, the payment of zakāt, the Fast of Ramaḍān and the Ḥajj to the House."

It is also narrated in the Ṣaḥīḥayn by Abū Hurayra ؓ that the Prophet ﷺ said: "Every good action made by man shall be multiplied by tenfold up to seven hundred-fold. Allāh ﷻ, says: 'Except for fasting, which is for Me, and I shall it reward it Myself; for a man renounces his food and his desire for My sake.' A fasting person has two joys: one when he breaks his fast, and the other when he meets his Lord. The odour of a fasting man's mouth is sweeter to Allāh than that of musk. Fasting is a shield."

الرَّابِعُ وَالْعِشْرُونَ مِنْ شعب الإيمان

الِاعْتِكَافُ لِقَوْلِهِ تَعَالَى ﴿وَعَهِدْنَا إِلَى إِبْرَاهِيمَ وَإِسْمَاعِيلَ أَنْ طَهِّرَا بَيْتِيَ لِلطَّائِفِينَ وَالْعَاكِفِينَ وَالرُّكَّعِ السُّجُودِ﴾.

وَلِحَدِيثِ عَائِشَةَ فِي الصَّحِيحَيْنِ أَنَّ النَّبِيَّ صلى الله عَلَيْهِ وَسلم كَانَ يَعْتَكِفُ الْعَشْرَ الْأَوَاخِرَ مِنْ رَمَضَانَ حَتَّى تَوَفَّاهُ اللَّهُ ثُمَّ اعْتَكَفَ أَزْوَاجُهُ مِنْ بَعْدِهِ.

وَلِما رُوِيَ عَنِ النَّبِيِّ صلى الله عَلَيْهِ وَسلم قَالَ ((من اعْتِكَفَ فُوَاقَ نَاقَةٍ فَكَأَنَّمَا أَعْتَقَ نَسَمَةً أَوْ رَقَبَةً)).

24. I'tikāf

Allāh Taʿālā says: "And We charged Ibrāhīm and Ismāʿīl, (saying), 'Purify My House for those who perform Ṭawāf and those who are staying (there) for worship and those who bow and prostrate (in prayer).'"[54]

It is narrated in the Ṣaḥīḥayn that ʿĀisha ؓ said that the Prophet

---

[54] Baqarah, 125.

ﷺ used to enter Iʿtikāf for the last ten days of Ramaḍān, until Allāh took his spirit. Afterwards, his wives did the same. The Prophet ﷺ said as narrated "whoever does Iʿtikāf for the time between two milkings (i.e. a moment) it is as though he has freed (from Hell) a soul."

الْخَامِس وَالْعشْرُونَ من شعب الإيمان

الْحَج لقَوْله تَعَالَى ﴿وَلِلَّهِ عَلَى النَّاسِ حِجُّ الْبَيْتِ مَنِ اسْتَطَاعَ إِلَيْهِ سَبِيلًا﴾ وَقَوله تَعَالَى ﴿وَأَذِّنْ فِي النَّاسِ بِالْحَجِّ يَأْتُوكَ رِجَالًا وَعَلَى كُلِّ ضَامِرٍ يَأْتِينَ مِنْ كُلِّ فَجٍّ عَمِيقٍ﴾ وَقَوله تَعَالَى ﴿وَأَتِمُّوا الْحَجَّ وَالْعُمْرَةَ لِلَّهِ﴾.

وَلِحَدِيث إِبْن عمر رَضِي الله عَنْهُمَا فِي الصَّحِيحَيْنِ ((بُنِيَ الإسلامُ عَلَى خَمْسٍ شَهَادَةِ أَن لَا إِله الا الله وَأَنَّ مُحَمَّدًا عَبْدُهُ وَرَسُوْلُهُ وإقامِ الصَّلَاةِ وإيْتاءِ الزَّكَاةِ وَصَوْمِ رَمَضَانَ وَحَجِّ الْبَيْتِ)).

وَحَدِيث عمر رَضِي الله عَنهُ فِي صَحِيح مُسلم قَالَ بَيْنَمَا نَحن جُلُوس عِنْد رَسُول الله صلى الله عَلَيْهِ وَسلم ((إِذْ جَاءَ رجلٌ فَقَالَ يَا مُحَمَّد! مَا الإسلام؟ قَالَ ((أَن تَشْهَدَ أَنْ لَا إِلَهَ إِلَّا اللهُ وَأَنَّ مُحَمَّدًا رَّسُوْلُ اللهِ وَأَنْ تُقِيمَ الصَّلَاةَ وتُؤْتِيَ الزَّكَاةَ وتَحُجَّ الْبَيْتَ وَتَعْتَمِرَ وَتَغْتَسِلَ مِنَ الْجَنَابَةِ وَتُتِمَّ الْوُضُوءَ وَتَصُوْمَ رَمَضَانَ)) قَالَ فَإِن فَعَلْتُ هذا، فَأَنا مُسلم؟ قَالَ ((نعم)) قَالَ صدقت ... فَذكر الحَدِيث.

وَرُوِيَ عَن أبي أُمَامَة الْبَاهِلِيّ رَضِي الله عَنهُ أن النَّبِي صلى الله عَلَيْهِ وَسلم قَالَ ((مَنْ لَمْ يَحْبِسْهُ مَرَضٌ أَوْ حَاجَةٌ ظَاهِرَةٌ أَو سُلْطَانٌ جَائِرٌ وَلَمْ يَحُجَّ فَلْيَمُتْ إِن شَاءَ يَهُودِيًّا وَإِنْ شَاءَ نَصْرَانِيًّا)).

25. Ḥajj

Allāh Taʿālā says: "And (due) to Allāh from the people is a Ḥajj to the House - for whoever is able to find thereto a way",[55] and: "Proclaim to the people the Ḥajj; they will come to you on foot and on every lean camel; they will come from every distant deep ravine",[56] and: "Complete the Ḥajj and the ʿUmra for Allāh". [57]

It is also narrated in the Ṣaḥīḥayn by Ibn ʿUmar ﷺ that the Prophet ﷺ said: "Islam is built on five things: Testimony that there is none worthy of worship except Allāh and that Muḥammed is the slave and messenger of Allḍāh, the establishment of ṣalāt, the payment of zakāt, the Fast of Ramaḍān and the Ḥajj to the House."

It is also narrated in Ṣaḥīḥ Muslim that ʿUmar ﷺ said: Once, when we were sitting in the presence of Rasulullāh ﷺ, a man came up and said, 'O Muḥammed! What is Islam?' And he replied, 'To testify that there is none worthy of worship except Allāh; and that Muḥammed is Rasulullāh, and to establish ṣalāt, to give the zakāt, to make Ḥajj and ʿUmra to the House, to perform ghusl for the state of janāba, to perform wuḍu correctly, and to fast during Ramaḍān.' 'If I do these things,' the man asked, 'then I will be a Muslim?' 'Yes', he replied. And the man said, 'You speak truly.'

It is narrated by Abū Umāma al-Bāhili that the Prophet ﷺ said, "Whoever is not prevented by an illness or any need, or a tyrant, and does not perform the Ḥajj: let him die a Jew if he wishes, or a Christian."

السَّادِس وَالْعِشْرُونَ من شعب الإيمان

الْجِهَاد لقَوْله تَعَالَى ﴿وَجَاهِدُوْا فِي اللهِ حَقَّ جِهَادِهِ﴾ وَقَوله تَعَالَى ﴿يُجَاهِدُوْنَ فِي سَبِيْلِ اللهِ وَلَا يَخَافُوْنَ لَوْمَةَ لَائِمٍ﴾ وَقَوله تَعَالَى ﴿قَاتِلُوْا الَّذِيْنَ يَلُوْنَكُمْ مِنَ الْكُفَّارِ وَلْيَجِدُوْا فِيكُمْ غِلْظَةً﴾ وَقَوله تَعَالَى ﴿يَا أَيُّهَا النَّبِيُّ حَرِّضِ الْمُؤْمِنِيْنَ عَلَى الْقِتَالِ﴾.

---

[55] Āl ʿImrān, 97.

[56] Ḥajj, 27.

[57] Baqarah, 196.

وَلِحَدِيث أبي هُرَيْرَة رَضِي الله عَنهُ فِي الصَّحِيحَيْنِ سُئِلَ رَسُول الله صلى الله عَلَيْهِ وَسلم أَي الأعمالِ أفضل؟ قَالَ ((الإيمانُ بِاللهِ وَرَسُولِهِ)) فَقيل ثمَّ مَاذَا؟ قَالَ ((الْجِهَادُ فِي سَبِيلِ اللهِ)) قيل ثمَّ مَاذَا؟ قَالَ ((حَجٌّ مَبْرُوْرٌ)).

وَحَدِيث عبد الله بن أبي أوفى رَضِي الله عَنْهُمَا فِي صَحِيح البُخَارِيّ ((لَا تَتَمَنَّوْا لِقَاءَ الْعَدُوِّ، وَسَلُوا اللهَ الْعَافِيَةَ فَإِذا لَقِيْتُمُوْهُمْ فَاصْبِرُوا وَاعْلَمُوْا أَنَّ الْجَنَّةَ تَحْتَ ظِلَالِ السُّيُوْفِ)).

26. Jihād

Allāh Taʿālā says: "Make Jihad in Allāh's cause as is His right",[58] and: "They strive in the cause of Allāh and do not fear the blame of a critic,"[59], and: "Fight those adjacent to you of the disbelievers and let them find in you, harshness",[60] and: "O Prophet, urge the believers to battle."[61]

It is narrated in the Ṣaḥīḥayn by Abū Hurayra ﷺ that the Prophet ﷺ was once asked "What is the finest of all acts?" He replied, "Īmān in Allāh and His Messenger." "And then what?" he was asked, and he answered, "Jihād in the path of Allāh." "Then what?" he was asked again, and he said, "An accepted Ḥajj."

It is narrated in Ṣaḥīḥ Bukhlāri by Ibn Abī Awfa ﷺ that the Prophet ﷺ said, "Do not look forward to encountering the enemy, rather ask Allāh for wellbeing. However, if you face them, then be steadfast, and know that Jannah is under the shade of swords."

السَّابِع وَالْعشْرُونَ من شعب الإيمان

المرابطة فِي سَبِيل الله عز وَجل لقَوْله تَعَالَى ﴿يَا أَيُّهَا الَّذِيْنَ آمَنُوا اصْبِرُوْا وَصَابِرُوْا

[58] Ḥajj, 78.
[59] Māida, 54.
[60] Tawba, 123.
[61] Anfāl, 65.

وَرَابِطُوْا وَاتَّقُوْا اللهَ﴾.

وَلِحَدِيث سهل بن سعد السَّاعِدِيّ رَضِي الله عَنهُ فِي صَحِيح البُخَارِيّ ((رِبَاطُ يَوْمٍ فِيْ سَبِيلِ اللهِ عَزَّ وَجَلَّ خَيْرٌ مِنَ الدُّنْيَا وَمَا فِيهَا وَمَوْضِعُ سَوطِ أَحَدِكُمْ مِنَ الْجَنَّةِ خَيْرٌ مِنَ الدُّنْيَا وَمَا عَلَيْهَا)).

والمرابطة تُنَزَّلُ مِن الْجِهَاد والقتال مَنْزِلَةَ الاِعْتِكَافِ فِي الْمَسَاجِدِ من الصَّلَاةِ لأَنَّ المرابط يُقيم فِي وَجهِ الْعَدُوِّ مثل قِيَامه مُتَأَهِّبًا مُسْتَعِدًّا لَهُ.

27. Ribāṭ - Protecting the Islamic Frontiers

Allāh Taʿālā says: "O you who have believed, persevere and endure and remain stationed and fear Allāh that you may be successful".[62]
It is narrated in Ṣaḥīḥ Bukhāri by Sahl bin Saʿd ﷺ that the Prophet ﷺ said that "To spend one day in the path of Allāh is better than the world and all it contains. The space of a man's whip in Jannah is better than the world and all that it contains."
Ribāṭ is to do Jihād and combat what Iʿtikāf in the masjid is to ṣalāt, since the man who does the former is staying constantly in the face of the enemy, and in total preparation.

الثَّامِن وَالْعشْرُونَ من شعب الإيمان

الثَّبَات لِلْعَدوّ وَترك الْفِرَار من الزَّحْف ﴿لقَوْله تَعَالَى إِذا لَقِيتُمْ فِئَةً فَاثْبُتُوْا﴾ وَقَوله تَعَالَى ﴿إِذَا لَقِيتُم الَّذين كَفَرُوْا زَحْفًا فَلَا تُوَلُّوْهُمْ الأَدْبَارَ وَمَنْ يُوَلِّهِمْ يَوْمَئِذٍ دُبُرَهُ إِلَّا مُتَحَرِّفًا لِقِتَالٍ أَوْ مُتَحَيِّزًا إِلَى فِئَةٍ فَقَدْ بَاءَ بِغَضَبٍ مِنَ اللهِ وَمَأْوَاهُ جَهَنَّمُ وَبِئْسَ الْمَصِيْرُ﴾

وَقَوله تَعَالَى ﴿يَا أَيُّهَا النَّبِيُّ حَرِّضِ الْمُؤمِنِيْنَ عَلَى الْقِتَالِ إِنْ يَكُنْ مِنْكُمْ عِشْرُوْنَ

[62] Āl ʿImrān, 200.

صَابِرُوْنَ يَغْلِبُوْا مِئَتَيْنِ﴾ الآيتين.

وَلِحَدِيثِ عَبْدِ اللهِ بْنِ أَبِيْ أَوْفَى رَضِيَ اللهُ عَنْهُمَا فِي صَحِيْحِ الْبُخَارِيِّ ((لَا تَتَمَنَّوْا لِقَاءَ الْعَدُوِّ وَسَلُوْا اللهَ الْعَافِيَةَ فَإِذَا لَقِيْتُمُوْهُمْ فَاصْبِرُوْا وَاعْلَمُوْا أَنَّ الْجَنَّةَ تَحْتَ ظِلَالِ السُّيُوْفِ)).

28. Determination in the face of an enemy, and not fleeing the fight

Allāh Taʿālā says: "When you encounter a company (from the enemy forces), stand firm",[63] and: "O you who have believed, when you meet those who disbelieve advancing (for battle), do not turn to them your backs (in flight). And whoever turns his back to them on such a day, unless swerving (as a strategy) for war or joining (another) company, has certainly returned with anger (upon him) from Allāh, and his refuge is Hell - and wretched is the destination.",[64] and: "O Prophet, urge the believers to battle. If there are among you twenty (who are) steadfast, they will overcome two hundred".[65]

It is narrated in Ṣaḥīḥ Bukhlāri by Ibn Abi Awfa ﷺ that the Prophet ﷺ said, "Do not look forward to encountering the enemy, rather ask Allāh for wellbeing. However, if you face them, then be steadfast, and know that Jannah is under the shade of swords."

التَّاسِع وَالْعِشْرُونَ من شعب الإيمانط

الْخمس من الْمغنم إلى الإمام وعماله على الْغَانِمين لقَوْله تَعَالَى ﴿وَأَعْلَمُوْا أَنَّمَا غَنِمْتُم مِنْ شَيْءٍ فَأَنَّ لِلّهِ خُمُسَهُ وَلِلرَّسُولِ وَلِذِي الْقُرْبَى وَالْيَتَامَى وَالْمَسَاكِيْنِ وَابْنِ السَّبِيْلِ إِنْ كُنْتُم آمَنْتُمْ بِاللهِ وَمَا أَنْزَلْنَا﴾ الأية وَقَوله تَعَالَى ﴿وَمَا كَانَ لِنَبِيٍّ أَنْ يَغُلَّ

[63] Anfāl, 45.
[64] Anfāl, 15-16.
[65] Anfāl, 65.

وَمَنْ يَغْلُلْ يَأْتِ بِمَا غَلَّ يَوْمَ الْقِيَامَةِ﴾.

وَلِحَدِيثِ إبْنِ عَبَّاسٍ رَضِيَ اللهُ عَنْهُمَا فِي الصَّحِيحَيْنِ عَنْ وَفْدِ عَبْدِ الْقَيْسِ ((آمُرُكُمْ بِأَرْبَعٍ، وأَنْهَاكُمْ عَنْ أَرْبَعٍ، آمُرُكُمْ: بِالإِيْمَانِ بِاللهِ وَحْدَهُ. أَتَدْرُوْنَ مَا الإيمانُ بِاللهِ وَحْدَهُ؟)) قَالُوْا: اللهُ وَرَسُوْلُهُ أَعْلَمُ. قَالَ ((شَهَادَةُ أَنْ لَا إِلَهَ إِلَّا اللهُ وَأَنَّ مُحَمَّدًا رَسُوْلُ اللهِ وإِقَامُ الصَّلَاةِ وَإِيْتَاءُ الزَّكَاةِ وَصِيَامُ رَمَضَانَ وَأَنْ تُعْطُوْا مِنَ الْمَغْنَمِ الْخُمُسَ وَأَنْهَاكُمْ عَنِ الحَنْتَمِ وَالدُّبَّاءِ والنَقِيْرِ وَالْمُزَفَّتِ. قَالَ: احْفَظُوْهُنَّ وَأَخْبِرُوْا بِهِنَّ مَنْ وَرَاءَكُمْ)).

29. Separating and paying the Khums from the spoils of war, to be paid to the ruler or his representative who supervises those who have taken the spoils

Allāh Taʿālā says: "And know that anything you obtain of war booty - then indeed, for Allāh is one fifth of it and for the Messenger and for (his) near relatives and the orphans, the needy, and the (stranded) traveler, if you have believed in Allāh and in that which We sent down to Our slave",[66] and: "It is not (attributable) to any prophet that he would act unfaithfully (in regard to war booty). And whoever betrays, (taking unlawfully), will come with what he took on the Day of Resurrection." [67]

It is also narrated in the Ṣaḥīḥayn by Ibn ʿAbbās ﵄ that the Prophet ﷺ told the delegation of ʿAbdul Qays, "I enjoin you to do four things, and to renounce four others. I enjoin you to believe in the One Allāh. Do you know what it is to believe in the One Allāh?" And they said, "Allāh and His Messenger know best." He said, "It is to testify that there is none worthy of worship except Allāh and that Muḥammed is Rasulullāh, to establish ṣalāt, to give the zakāt, to fast Ramaḍān, and to give one-fifth of any spoils of war. And I

---

[66] Anfāl, 41.
[67] Āl ʿImrān, 161.

enjoin you to renounce four other things, which are Ḥantam, dubbā', naqīr and muzaffat (types of utensils used for alcohol). Observe these orders, and speak of them to the people you know."

الثَّلَاثُونَ من شعب الإيمان

الْعتق بِوَجْه التَّقَرُّب إلى الله عز وَجل لقَوْله تَعَالَى ﴿فَلَا اقْتَحَمَ الْعَقَبَةَ وَمَا أَدْرَاكَ مَا الْعقبَة فَكُّ رَقَبَة﴾.

وَلِحَدِيث أبي هُرَيْرَة رَضِي الله عَنهُ فِي الصَّحِيحَيْنِ ((من أعتق رَقَبَة أعتق الله بِكُل عُضْو مِنْهَا عضوا من أَعْضَائِهِ من النَّار حَتَّى فرجه بفرجه)).

30. Freeing slaves, as an act of worship.

Allāh Ta'ālā says: "But he has not broken through the difficult pass. And what can make you know what is (breaking through) the difficult pass? It is the freeing of a slave." [68]

It is also narrated in the Ṣaḥīḥayn by Abū Hurayra ﷺ that the Prophet ﷺ said, "Whoever frees the limbs of a slave, Allāh will free the same limbs for him from the Fire even his private parts in place of the slave's private parts."

الْحَادِي وَالثَّلَاثُونَ من شعب الإيمان

الْكَفَّارَات الْوَاجِبَات بالجنايات وَهِي بِالْكتاب وَالسّنة أَربع كَفَّارَات: كَفَّارَة الْقَتْل، وَكَفَّارَة الظِّهَار، وَكَفَّارَة الْيَمين، وَكَفَّارَة الْمَسِيس فِي صَوْم رَمَضَان، وَمِمَّا يقرب مِنْهَا مَا يجب باسم الْفِدْيَة، لأنها إِمَّا عَن ذَنْب سبق، أَو يُرَاد بِهِ التَّقَرُّب إلى الله تَعَالَى بشيء، يَعْنِي إِثْر أَمْر قد وَقع، ذَنبا كَانَ أَو غير ذَنْب.

---

[68] Balad, 11-13.

31. The atonement (kaffārāt) which must be paid for criminal offences

According to the Book and the Sunna, there are four atonements: the atonement for murder, the atonement for Ẓihār (a type of divorce), the atonement for a broken oath, and the atonement for intercourse while fasting in Ramaḍān. There are also similar obligatory penalties known as fidya (or redemptions), which are for a previous sin, or which may be done to bring one closer to Allāh Taʿālā after something which has happened, whether or not it was of a sinful nature.

الثَّانِي وَالثَّلَاثُونَ من شعب الإيمان

الإيفاء بِالْعُقُودِ لقَوْله تَعَالَى ﴿أَوفوا بِالْعُقُودِ﴾. وَقَالَ إِبْن عَبَّاس رَضِي الله عَنْهُمَا يَعْنِي مَا أحل الله وَمَا حرم وَمَا فرض وَمَا حد فِي الْقُرْآن كُله. ﴿وَقَوله تَعَالَى يُوفون بِالنذرِ﴾ وَقَوله تَعَالَى ﴿وليوفوا نذورهم﴾ وَقَوله تَعَالَى ﴿وَمِنْهُم من عَاهَدَ الله﴾ وَقَوله تَعَالَى ﴿وأوفوا بِعَهْد الله إِذا عاهدتم وَلَا تنقضوا الإيمان بعد توكيدها﴾ الاية.

وَلِحَدِيث عبد الله بن مَسْعُود رَضِي الله عَنهُ فِي صَحِيح البُخَارِيّ ((لكُل غادر لِوَاء يَوْم الْقِيَامَة يُقَال هَذِه غدرة فلَان)) وَحَدِيث عبد الله بن عَمْرو رَضِي الله عَنْهُمَا فِي الصَّحِيحَيْنِ ((أَربع من كن فِيهِ كَانَ منافقا خَالِصا وَمن كَانَت فِيهِ خصْلَة مِنْهُنَّ كَانَت فِيهِ خصْلَة من النِّفَاق حَتَّى يدعهَا إِذا حدث كذب وَإِذا عَاهَدَ غدر وَإِذا وعد أخلف

وَإِذا خَاصم فجر)) وَحَدِيث عقبَة بن عَامر الْجُهَنِيّ فِي صَحِيح مُسلم ((إِن أَحَق الشُّرُوط أَن يُوفى بِهِ مَا استحللتم بِهِ الْفروج)).

32. Fulfilling one's undertakings

Allāh Ta'ālā says: "Fulfill your undertakings." [69] Ibn 'Abbas ؓ said, "This refers to one's promise to observe Allāh's permissions, prohibitions, commands and limits, as set out in the Qur'ān." Allāh Ta'ālā says also: "Those who fulfill their vows",[70] and: "Let them fulfill the vows which they have made", [71] and: "Among them are such as vow unto Allāh",[72] and: "Be true to your bond with Allāh whenever you make a pledge, and do not break your oaths after having confirmed them." [73]

It is also narrated in Ṣaḥīḥ Bukhāri by Ibn Mas'ūd ؓ that the Prophet said, "On the Day of Reserruction, every treacherous man will bear a banner, and it will be said, "Behold the treachery of so and so!'"

It is also narrated in the Ṣaḥīḥayn by Ibn 'Amr ؓ that the Prophet ﷺ said, "There are four things which make a man a pure hypocrite if they are all present within him, and a partial hypocrite if only one is present: if he lies when he speaks, if he commits and then cheats, if he makes promises which he breaks, and when he argues he deviates from the truth."

It is also narrated in Ṣaḥīḥ Muslim by 'Uqba ibn 'Āmir ؓ that the Prophet ﷺ said, "The condition which one is most obliged to fulfill is that which one enters upon at the time of marriage."

الثَّالِثُ وَالثَّلَاثُونَ مِن شعب الإيمان

تعديد نعم الله عزوجل وَمَا يجب من شكرها لقَوْله تَعَالَى ﴿قل الْحَمد لله﴾ وَقَوله تَعَالَى ﴿وَإِن تعدوا نِعْمَة الله لَا تحصوها﴾ وَقَوله تَعَالَى ﴿واما بِنِعْمَة رَبك فَحدث﴾ وَقَوله تَعَالَى ﴿فاذكروني أذكركم وأشكروا لي وَلَا تكفرون﴾ وَغير ذَلِكِ

---

[69] Māida, 1.
[70] Insān, 7.
[71] Ḥajj, 29.
[72] Tawba, 75.
[73] Naḥl, 91.

مِمَّا من الله تَعَالَى على عباده وَذكرهمْ بهَا فِي كِتَابه.

وَلِحَدِيث ابي ذَر رَضِي الله عَنهُ فِي صَحِيح البُخَارِيّ قَالَ كَانَ رَسُول الله صلى الله عَلَيْهِ وَسلم إِذا أَخذ مضجعه من اللَّيْل قَالَ ((بِاسْمِك أَمُوت وَأَحْيَا)) وَإِذا اسْتَيْقَظ قَالَ ((الْحَمد الله الَّذِي أحياني بَعْدَمَا اماتني واليه النشور)).

وَحَدِيث صُهَيْب رَضِي الله عَنهُ فِي صَحِيح مُسلم ((عجبا لِأَمر الْمُؤمن إِن أمْرَهْ كُله خير وَلَيْسَ ذَاك لأحدٍ إِلَّا لِلْمُؤمنِ إِن أَصَابَته سراء شكر فَكَانَ خيرا لَهُ وَإِن أصابته ضراء صَبر فَكَانَ خيرا لَهُ)).

وَبِه قَالَ الْبَيْهَقِيّ قَالَ أَنا الْحَافِظ ابو عبد الله قَالَ أنشدني أبو عبد الله بن أبي ذهل قَالَ أنشد ابو الْحسن الْكِنْدِيّ القَاضِي:

إِذا كنت فِي نعْمَة فارعها ... فَإِن الْمعاصِي تزيل النعم

قَالَ أخبرنَا أبو عبد الرحمن السّلميّ قَالَ سَمِعت الْحُسَيْن بن يُوسُف الْقزْوِينِي قَالَ سَمِعت أَبَا بكر أَحْمد بن إسحاق قَالَ سَمِعت الْجُنَيْد قَالَ سَمِعت السّري يَقُول الشُّكْر نعْمَة وَالشُّكْر على النعم نعْمَة إِلَى أن لَا يتناهى الشُّكْر إِلَى قَرَار. وَقد قَالَ الإِمَام الشَّافِعِي رَحمَه الله فِي أول كتاب الرسَالَة الْحَمد لله الَّذِي لَا يُؤَدِّي شكر نعْمَة من نعمه إِلَّا بِنِعْمَة مِنْهُ توجب على مؤدي ذَلِك الشُّكْر وَبِه. أَنا الْبَيْهَقِيّ قَالَ أنبانا ابو الْقَاسِم أنبأ أَحْمد بن سلمَان أَنا إِبْن إبي الدُّنْيَا إِلَخ. قَالَ فأنشدنا مَحْمُود الْوراق:

لَئِن كَانَ شكري نعْمَة الله نعْمَة ... عَليّ لَهُ فِي مثلهَا يجب الشُّكْر

فَكيف يَصح الشُّكْر إِلَّا بفضله ... وَإِن طَالَتْ الأيام واتصل الْعُمر

إِذا مس بالسراء عَم سرورها ... وَإِن مس بالضراء أعقبها الأجر

وَمَا مِنْهُمَا إِلَّا لَهُ فِيهِ مِنْهُ ... تضيق بهَا الأوهام وَالْبر وَالْبَحْر

وَأَخْبرنَا من غير رِوَايَة الْبَيْهَقِيّ جمَاعَة بَيْتَيْنِ فَقَط:

إِذا كَانَ شكري نعْمَة الله نعْمَة ... عَليّ لَهُ فِي مثلهَا يجب الشُّكْر

فَمَا لي عذر أَنِّي مقصر ... وعذري إقراري بِأَن لَيْسَ لي عذر

33. Recounting the blessings of Allāh, and giving the necessary thanks

Allāh Taʿālā says: "Say: Praised be to Allāh!",[74] and: "And if you should count the favor of Allāh, you could not enumerate them.",[75] and: "But as for the favor of your Lord, report (it).",[76] and: "Remember Me, and I will remember you; give thanks to Me, and reject Me not".[77] Allāh Taʿālā mentions other such verses concerning Allāh's gifts to His slaves, and His reminding them thereof.

It is narrated in Ṣaḥīḥ Bukhāri by Abū Dhar ﷺ that the Prophet said, "Whenever Rasulullāh ﷺ went to bed at night, he would say, 'In Your name do I die and am I given life again,' and when he awoke, he would say, 'Praised be Allāh Who gave me life after He caused me to die. And unto Him shall be the resurrection'."

It is narrated in Ṣaḥīḥ Muslim by Ṣuhayb ﷺ "The affairs of a believer are astonishing, and are all good; that is when good comes to him he gives thanks, while when something bad comes he is patient, which is good for him also."

Abū Ḥasan al-Kindi recited the following lines:

If you have been given blessings,
then look after them for sins do away with blessings.

Al-Junayd said, "I once heard al-Sari saying, 'Because to give thanks for blessings is in itself a blessing, one can never cease to give thanks.'" Imām al-Shāfiʿī writes at the beginning of his Risāla "Praised be to Allāh, Who, whenever He is thanked for one of His

---

[74] Naml, 59.

[75] Ibrahīm, 34.

[76] Duha, 11.

[77] Baqara, 152.

blessings, provides another blessing, which in turn obliges one to thank Him again!"

According to Ibn Abi Dunya, the following couplets were composed by Maḥmūd al-Warraq:

If my thanking Allāh for His blessings is a blessing,
then I must thank Him in the same measure again.
How can one thank Him except by His grace
as time goes on, and life goes by?
If a good thing comes, I rejoice heartily;
if a bad one comes, I receive a reward.
In both cases He gives me a gift too large
for the minds of men, and the land and sea.

In another version, the last three verses are replaced by the following:

My only excuse is that- I am inadequate
but my excuse is a confession that I have no excuse.

الرَّابِع وَالثَّلَاثُونَ من شعب الإيمان

حفظ اللِّسَان عَمَّا لَا يحْتَاج اليه وَيدخل فِيهِ الْكَذِب والغيبة والنميمة وَالْفُحْش. إِذْ الْقُرْآن وَالسّنة مشحونان بذلك كَقَوْلِه تَعَالَى ﴿والصادقين والصادقات﴾ وَقَوله تَعَالَى ﴿يَا أيها الَّذين آمنُوا اتَّقوا الله وَكُونُوا مَعَ الصَّادِقين﴾ وَقَوله تَعَالَى ﴿وَلَا تقف مَا لَيْسَ لَك بِهِ علم﴾ وَقَوله تَعَالَى ﴿فَمن أظلم مِمَّن كذب على الله وَكذب بِالصِّدق إِذْ جَاءَهُ﴾ وَقَوله تَعَالَى ﴿وَالَّذِي جَاءَ بِالصِّدق وَصدق بِهِ أُولَئِكَ هم المتقون﴾ وَقَوله تَعَالَى ﴿إِن الَّذين يفترون على الله الْكَذِب لَا يفلحون﴾.

وَلِحَدِيث عبد الله بن مَسْعُود رَضِي الله عَنهُ فِي الصَّحِيحَيْنِ ((إِن الصدْق يهدي إِلى الْبر وَإِن الْبر يهدي إِلى الْجنَّة وَإِن الرجل ليصدق حَتَّى يكْتب عِنْد الله صديقا وَإِن الْكَذِب يهدي إِلى الْفُجُور وَإِن الْفُجُور يهدي إِلى النَّار وَإِن الرجل

ليكذب حَتَّى يكْتب عِنْد الله كذابا)).

وَحَدِيث سهل بن سعد رَضِي الله عَنهُ فِي صَحِيح مُسلم ((من يضمن لي مَا بَين لحييْهِ وَمَا بَين فَخذيهِ أضمن لَهُ الْجنَّة)).

وَحَدِيث أبي شُرَيْح الْخُزَاعِيّ فِيهِ أيضا ((من كَانَ يُؤمن بِاللَّه وَالْيَوْم الآخر فَلْيقل خيرا أَوْ ليصمت)).

34. Holding one's tongue from unnecessary speech, which includes lying, slandering, backbiting and obscenity

The Qurʾān and the Sunna are full of guidance in this regard. For instance, Allāh Taʿālā says: "Truthful men and truthful women",[78] and: "O you who believe! Fear Allāh, and be with those that true,",[79]and: "Do not concern yourself with that of which you have no ʿilm",[80] and: "Who is more-evil than he who invents lies about Allāh and gives the lie to the truth when it comes to him? Is not hell the abode of all who disbelieve? But he who brings the truth, and he who accepts it as true — such are the Allāh fearing",[81] and: "Those who invent lies about Allāh shall not succeed." [82]

It is narrated in the Ṣaḥīḥayn by Ibn Masʿūd ﵁ that the Prophet ﷺ said, "Truthfulness leads to goodness, and goodness leads to Jannah. A man tells the truth until Allāh records him as being a man of truthfulness. Lying, however, leads to wickedness, and wickedness leads to the Fire; a man tells lies until Allāh records him as a liar."

It is narrated in Ṣaḥīḥ Muslim by Sahl ibn Saʿd ﵁ that the Prophet ﷺ said, "Whoever can promise me that he will be virtuous that which is between his jaws, and that which is between his thighs; I promise that he will go to Jannah."

---

78 Aḥzāb, 35.

79 Tawba, 119.

80 Isrā, 36.

81 Zumar, 31-32

82 Yūnus, 69.

It is also narrated in Ṣaḥīḥ Muslim by Abū Shurayḥ al-Khuzāʿi that the Prophet ﷺ said, "Anyone who believes in Allāh and the Last Day should speak with goodness, or remain silent."

الْخَامِس وَالثَّلَاثُونَ من شعب الإيمان

الأمانات وَمَا يجب فِيهَا من أدائها إِلَى أَهلها لقَوْله تَعَالَى ﴿إِن الله يَأْمُركُمْ أَن تُؤَدُّوا الأمانات إِلَى أَهلهَا﴾ وَقَوله تَعَالَى ﴿فليؤد الَّذِي ائْتمن أَمَانَته﴾.

وَلِحَدِيث أبي هُرَيْرَة رَضِي الله عَنهُ ((أد الامانة إِلَى من ائتمنك وَلَا تخن من خانك))

ولحديثه فِي الصَّحِيحَيْنِ ((ثَلَاث من كن فِيهِ فَهُوَ مُنَافِق وَإِن صَامَ وَصلى وَزعم أَنه مُسلم إِذا حدث كذب وَإِذا وعد أخلف وَإِذا ائْتمن خَان)).

35. Holding things in trust for others

Allāh Taʿālā says: "Allāh commands you to deliver what you have been entrusted to those who are entitled to it",[83] and: "Let him who is entrusted, fulfil his trust." [84]

According to Abū Hurayra ؓ, the Prophet ﷺ said, "Give what you hold in trust back to the person who entrusted you with it, and do not betray anyone, even should he have betrayed you."

It is narrated in the Ṣaḥīḥayn by Abū Hurayra ؓ that the Prophet ﷺ said, "There are three things which, if present in a man show him to be a hypocrite, even if he prays, fasts and claims to be a Muslim: if when speaking, he lies, if when making a promise, he breaks his promise, and if when entrusted with anything, he betrays his trust."

---

[83] Nisā, 58.

[84] Baqara, 283.

السَّادِسُ وَالثَّلَاثُونَ من شعب الإيمان

تَحْرِيمُ قتل النُّفُوس والجنايات عَلَيْهَا لقَوْله تَعَالَى ﴿وَمن يقتل مُؤمنا مُتَعَمدا فَجَزَاؤُهُ جَهَنَّمُ خَالِدا فِيهَا وَغَضب الله عَلَيْهِ﴾ الآية وَلقَوْله تَعَالَى ﴿لَا تقتلُوا أنفسكم...﴾ الآيات.

وَلِحَدِيث عبد الله بن مَسْعُود رَضِي الله عَنهُ فِي الصَّحِيحَيْنِ ((قتال الْمُسلم كفر وسبابه فسوق)).

وَحَدِيثه فِي صَحِيحِ البُخَارِيّ ((أول مَا يقْضى بَين النَّاس يَوْم الْقِيَامَة فِي الدِّمَاء)).

وَلِحَدِيث إبْن عمر رَضِي الله عَنْهُمَا فِي الصَّحِيحَيْنِ ((لَا يزَال الْمُسلم فِي فسحه من دينه مَا لم يصب دَمًا حَرَامًا)).

36. The prohibition of murder and other crimes

Allāh Taʿālā says: "Whoever deliberately murders a believer shall be rewarded with Jahannam, where he shall remain forever, and Allāh's wrath shall be upon him."[85]

It is narrated in the Ṣaḥīḥayn by Ibn Masʿūd ؓ that the Prophet ﷺ said, "To murder a Muslim is kufr, and to insult him is wickedness."

It is also narrated in the Ṣaḥīḥayn by Ibn Masʿūd ؓ that the Prophet ﷺ said, "The first injustices to be put right on the Day of Reserruction will be those involving bloodshed."

It is narrated in the Ṣaḥīḥayn by Ibn ʿUmar ؓ that the Prophet ﷺ said, "A Muslim remains firmly attached to his Dīn as long as he has not spilt forbidden blood."

السَّابِعُ وَالثَّلَاثُونَ من شعب الإيمان

تَحْرِيم الْفروج وَمَا يجب فِيهَا من التعفف لقَوْله تَعَالَى ﴿وَيَحْفَظُوْا فُرُوْجَهُمْ﴾ وَقَوله

---

[85] Nisā, 93.

تَعَالَى ﴿وَيَحْفَظْنَ فُرُوجَهُنَّ﴾ وَقَوْله تَعَالَى ﴿وَالَّذِينَ هُمْ لِفُرُوجِهِمْ حَافِظُونَ﴾ وَقَوْله تَعَالَى ﴿وَلَا تَقْرَبُوا الزِّنَا إِنَّهُ كَانَ فَاحِشَةً وَسَاءَ سَبِيلًا﴾.

وَلِحَدِيث ابي هُرَيْرَة رَضِي الله عَنْهُ فِي الصَّحِيحَيْنِ ((لَا يَزْنِي الزَّانِي حِين يَزْنِي وَهُوَ مُؤْمِن، وَلَا يسرق السَّارِق حِين يسرق وَهُوَ مُؤْمِن، وَلَا يشرب الخَمْر حِين يشربها وَهُوَ مُؤْمِن، لَا ينتهب نهبة ذَات شرف يرفع الْمُؤْمِنُونَ إِلَيْهِ فِيهَا أبصارهم حِين ينتهبها وَهُوَ مؤمن)).

37. Saving oneself from aldultery by adopting chastity

Allāh Taʿālā says: "Men who guard their private parts", [86] and: "Women who guard their private parts,"[87] and: "Those who guard their private parts,"[88] and: "Do not come near adultery, for it is a foulness and an evil way."[89]

It is narrated in the Ṣaḥīḥayn by Abū Hurayra ﷺ that the Prophet ﷺ said, "The adulterer is not a believer while he is committing adultery. The drinker of wine is not a believer while he is drinking wine. The thief is not a believer while he is stealing. The plunderer is not a believer while he is plundering and the people are looking to him."

الثَّامِن وَالثَّلَاثُونَ من شعب الإيمان

قبض الْيَد عَن الاموال وَيدخل فِيهَا تَحْرِيم السَّرقَة وَقطع الطَّرِيق وَأكل الرشا وَأكل مَالا يسْتَحقّهُ شرعا لقَوْله تَعَالَى ﴿وَلَا تَأْكُلُوا أموالكم بَيْنكُم بِالْبَاطِلِ﴾ وَقَوْله تَعَالَى ﴿فبظلم من الَّذين هادوا حرمنا عَلَيْهِم طَيِّبَات أحلت لَهُم وبصدهم

---

[86] Nūr, 30.
[87] Nūr, 31.
[88] Mu'minūn, 5.
[89] Isrā, 32.

عَن سَبِيل الله كثيرا واخذهم الرِّبَا وَقد نهوا عَنهُ وأكلهم أموال النَّاس بِالْبَاطِلِ﴾ وَقَوله تَعَالَى ﴿ويل لِلْمُطَفِّفِينَ﴾ وَقَوله تَعَالَى ﴿وأوفوا الْكَيْل إِذا كلتم وزنوا بالقسطاس الْمُسْتَقيم﴾.

وَلِحَدِيث عبد الرَّحْمَن بن إِبي بكرَة فِي الصَّحِيحَيْنِ عَن أَبيه رَضِي الله عَنْهُمَا قَالَ خَطَبنَا رَسُول الله صلى الله عَلَيْهِ وَسلم بمنى فَقَالَ ((إِن دماءكم وأموالكم وأعراضكم عَلَيْكُم حرَام)) الحَدِيث.

38. Not appropriating the property of others includes the prohibition of theft, highway robbery, usury (interest) and consuming any money or property to which one is not entitled under Islamic Law

Allāh Ta'ālā says: "Devour not one another's possessions wrongfully", [90] and: "For the injustice committed by those who were Jews did We deny unto them some of the good things of life which had formerly been permitted them, and for their frequent obstruction of the way of Allāh, and their taking of usury even though it was forbidden them, and their wrongful devouring of other people's wealth",[91] and: "Woe bet to those who give short measure!"[92] and: "Give full measure whenever you give measure, and weigh with a balance that is fair." [93]
It is narrated in the Ṣaḥīḥayn by Abū Bakra ﷺ that Rasulullāh ﷺ once preached a sermon before us at Mina, and declared, 'Your lives, your possessions, and your honour are inviolable'."

---

[90] Baqara, 188.
[91] Nisā, 160.
[92] Mutaffifīn, 1.
[93] Isrā, 35.

التَّاسِع وَالثَّلَاثُونَ من شعب الإيمان

وجوب التورع فِي المطاعم والمشارب والإجتناب عَمَّا لَا يحل مِنْهَا لقَوْله تَعَالَى ﴿حرمت عَلَيْكُم الْميتَة وَالدَّم وَلحم الْخِنْزِير وَمَا أهل لغير الله بِهِ والمنخنقة﴾ الْآيَة. وَقَوله تَعَالَى ﴿قل لَا أجد فِيمَا أوحي إِلَى محرما على طاعم يطعمهُ إِلا أَن يكون ميتَة أَوْ دَمًا مسفوحا أَوْ لحم خِنْزِير فَإِنَّهُ رِجْس أَوْ فسقا أهل لغير الله بِهِ﴾ وَقَوله تَعَالَى ﴿إِنما الْخمر وَالْميسر والأنصاب والأزلام رِجْس من عمل الشَّيْطَان فَاجْتَنبُوهُ﴾ الْآيَات. وَقَوله تَعَالَى ﴿يسئلونك عَن الْخمر وَالْميسر قل فيهمَا إِثم كَبِير﴾ الْآيَة. فَأثْبت فِيهَا الإِثم وَقَالَ فِي آيَة أُخرى ﴿قل إِنما حرم رَبِّي الْفَوَاحِش مَا ظهر مِنْهَا وَمَا بطن والإِثم وَالْبَغي بِغَيْر الْحق﴾ فَحرم الإِثم نصا. وَيُقَال إِن الإِثم اسْم من أَسمَاء الْخمر وينشده:

شربت الاثم حَتَّى ضل عَقْلِي ... كَذَاك الاثم يذهب بالعقول

وَلحَدِيث عَائِشَة رَضِي الله عَنْهَا فِي الصَّحِيحَيْنِ سُئِلَ رَسُول الله صلى الله عَلَيْهِ وَسلم عَن البتع. فَقَالَ ((كل شراب أسكر فَهُوَ حرَام)).

وَحَدِيث ابْن عمر رَضِي الله عَنْهُمَا فِي صَحِيح مُسلم ((كل مُسكر خمر وكل خمر حرَام)).

وَحَدِيثه فِي الصَّحِيحَيْنِ ((من شرب الْخمر فِي الدُّنْيَا ثمَّ لم يتب مِنْهَا حرمهَا فِي الآخرة)).

وَحَدِيث أبي هُرَيْرَة رَضِي الله عَنهُ فيهمَا أُتِي رَسُول الله صلى الله عَلَيْهِ وَسلم لَيْلَة أسري بِهِ بإيلياء بقدحين من خمر وَلبن فَنظر اليهما ثمَّ اخذ اللَّبن فَقَالَ لَهُ جِبْرِيل عَلَيْهِ السَّلَام الْحَمد لله الَّذِي هداك للفطرة لَو أخذت الْخمر لغوت أمتك.

وَلحديثه فيهمَا ((وَلَا يشرب الْخمر الشَّارِب حِين يشربهَا وَهُوَ مُؤمن)) الحَدِيث.

وَبه أنا الْبَيْهَقِيّ بِإِسْنَادِهِ عَن الْحسن قَالَ جَاءَ رجل بنبيذ إِلى أحب خلق الله إِلَيْهِ أفسده يَعْنِي الْعقل. وَقيل لبَعض الْعَرَب لم لَا تشرب النَّبِيذ؟ فَقَالَ وَالله مَا أرضى عَقْلِي صَحِيحا، فَكيف أَدخل اليه مَا يُفْسِدهُ.

وَعَن الحكم بن هِشَام انه قَالَ لِابْنِ لَهُ يَا بني إياك والنبيذ فَإِنَّهُ قيء فِي شدقك، وسلح على عقبك، وحد فِي ظهرك، وَتَكون ضحكة للصبيان وأسيرا للديان.

وَعَن بعض الْحُكَمَاء أَنه قَالَ لِابْنِهِ يَا بني! مَا يَدْعُوك الى النَّبِيذ؟ قَالَ يهضم طَعَامي. قَالَ وَالله! يَا بني هُوَ لدينك أهضم. وَعَن عبد الله بن إِدْرِيس:

كل شراب مُسكر كَثِيره ... من تَمْرَة اَوْ عِنَب عصيره

فَإِنَّهُ محرم يسيره ... إِنِّي لكم من شَره نذيره

وَعَن أبي بكر بن أبي الدُّنْيَا أَنه أنشده أَبوه:

وَإِذا النَّبِيذ على النَّبِيذ شربته ... أزرى بِدينِك مَعَ ذهَاب الدِّرْهَم

وأنشدنا الْحُسَيْن بن عبد الرَّحْمَن:

أرى كل قوم يحفظون حريمهم ... وَلَيْسَ لاصحاب النَّبِيذ حَرِيم

إِذا جئتهم حيوك ألفا ورحبوا ... وَإِن غبت عَنْهُم سَاعَة فذميم

أَخَاهُم إِذا مَا دارت الكأس بَينهم ... وَكلهمْ رث الْوِصَال سؤوم

فَهَذَا ثنائي لم أقل بِجَهَالَة ... وَلَكِن بِحَال الْفَاسِقين عليم

وَفِي صَحِيح مُسلم وَغَيره من حَدِيث أبي هُرَيْرَة رَضِي الله عَنهُ ((أَيهَا النَّاس إِن الله طيب لَا يقبل إِلَّا طيبا وَإِن الله تَعَالَى أمر الْمُؤمنِينَ بِمَا أمر بِهِ الْمُرْسلين. فَقَالَ: ﴿يَا ايها الرُّسُل كلوا من الطَّيِّبَات وَاعْمَلُوا صَالحا إنى بِمَا تَعْمَلُونَ عليم﴾ وَقَالَ: ﴿يَا أَيهَا الَّذين امنوا كلوا من طَيِّبَات مَا رزقناكم واشكروا الله إِن كُنْتُم إِيَّاه تَعْبُدُونَ﴾ ثمَّ ذكر الرجل يُطِيل السّفر أَشْعَث إغبر يمد يَدَيْهِ إِلَى السَّمَاء يَا

رب يَا رب! ومطعمة حرَام، وملبسه حرَام، ومشربه حرَام، وغذي بالحرام، فأنى يُسْتَجَاب لَهُ)).

وَفِي الصَّحِيحَيْنِ من حَدِيث النُّعْمَان بن بشير رَضِي الله عَنهُ ((إِن الْحَلَال بَين وَإِن الْحَرَام بَين وَبَين ذَلِك مُشْتَبَهَات لَا يعلمهَا كثير من النَّاس فَمن اتَّقى الشُّبُهَات فقد اسْتَبْرَأَ لعرضه وَدينه وَمن وَقع فِي الشُّبُهَات وَقع فِي الْحَرَام كَالرَّاعِي يرْعَى حول الْحمى يُوشك أَن يَقع فِيهِ أَلا وَإِن لكل ملك حمى وَحمى الله فِي الأرض مَحَارمه)).

وَفِي الصَّحِيحَيْنِ من حَدِيث أَبي هُرَيْرَة ((إِنِّي لأنقلب إِلَى أَهلي فأجد التمرة سَاقِطَة على فِرَاشِي أَو فِي بَيْتِي فأرفعها لأكلها ثمَّ أخشى أَن تكون من الصدقة فألقيها)).

وَفِي صَحِيح البُخَارِيّ عَن عَائِشَة رَضِي الله عَنْهَا قَالَت كَانَ لأبي بكر غُلَام يخرج لَهُ الْخراج وَكَانَ أَبُو بكر يَأْكُل من خراجه. فجَاء يَوْمًا بِشَيْء فَأكل مِنْهُ أَبُو بكر. فَقَالَ: لَهُ الْغُلَام أَتَدْرِي مَا هَذَا؟ فَقَالَ أَبُو بكر رَضِي الله عَنهُ وَمَا هُوَ؟ قَالَ كنت تكهنت لإنْسَان فِي الْجَاهِلِيَّة. وَمَا أحسن الكهانة إِلَّا أَنِّي خدعته فلقيني فأعطاني بذلك فَهَذَا الَّذِي أكلت مِنْهُ. قَالَت: فَأَدْخل أَبُو بكر يَده، فقاء كل شَيْء فِي بَطْنه.

وَعَن زيد بن أَسلم أَن عمر بن الْخطاب رَضِي الله عَنهُ شرب لَبَنًا فأعجبه. فَقَالَ لَلَّذِي سقَاهُ من أَيْن لَك هَذَا؟ اللَّبن فَأخْبرهُ انه ورد على مَاء قد سَمَّاهُ فَإِذا نعم من نعم الصَّدَقَة وهم يسقون فحلبوه لي من أَلْبَانهَا فَجَعَلته فِي سقائي وَهُوَ هَذَا فَأَدْخل عمر يَده فاستقاءه. وَعَن عَليّ رَضِي الله عَنهُ فِي طيب مطعمه انه كَانَ يجاء بخبزه فِي جراب من الْمَدِينَة.

أنبأنَا الْبَيْهَقِيّ بإِسْنَادِهِ عَن بشر بن الْحَارِث قَالَ قَالَ يُوسُف إبْن أسباط إِذا تعبد الشَّاب يَقُول إِبْلِيس أنْظُرُوا من أَيْن مطعمه فَإِن كَانَ مطعمه مطعم سوء قَالَ

دَعوه لَا تشتغلوا بِهِ دَعوه يجْتَهد وَينصب فقد كفاكم نَفسه.

وَعَن حُذَيْفَة المرعشي أنه نظر إلى النَّاس يتبادرون إلى الصَّف الأول. فَقَالَ يَنْبَغِي أن يتبادروا إلى أكل خبز الْحَلَال. وَعَن الفضيل بن عِيَاض قَالَ سُئِلَ سُفْيَان الثَّوْرِيّ عَن فضل الصَّف الأول فَقَالَ أنْظُر كسرتك الَّتِي تأكل من أيْنَ تأكلها وصل فِي الصَّفّ الاخير. وَعنهُ أَيْضا أنْظُر درهمك من أَيْن هُوَ وصل فِي الصَّفّ الاخير.

وَعَن سري السَّقطِي أنه كَانَ لَا يَأْكُل من بقل السوَاد وَلَا من ثمره وَلَا من شَيْء يعلم أنه مِنْهُ ويشدد فِي ذَلِك وَكَانَ غَايَة فِي الْوَرع وَمَعَ ذَلِك قَالَ كنت بطرسوس وَكَانَ معي فِي الدَّار فتيَان يتعبدون وَكَانَ فِي الدَّار تنور يخبزون فِيهِ فانكسر التَّنور مضملت بدله من مَالِي فتورعوا أَن يخبزوا فِيهِ.

وَعنهُ قَالَ كَانَ أَبُو يُوسُف الغسولي يلْزم الثغر ويغزو فَكَانَ إِذا غزا مَعَ النَّاس ودخلوا بِلَاد الرّوم أكل أصحابه من ذَبَائِحهم وفواكههم وَهُوَ لَا يَأْكُل فَيُقَال لَهُ يَا أَبَا يُوسُف أتشك أنه حَلَال فَيَقُول لَا فَيُقَال لَهُ فَكل من الْحَلَال فَيَقُول إِنَّمَا الزّهْد فِي الْحَلَال.

وَعَن السّري قَالَ رجعت من بعض الْمَغَازِي فَرَأَيْت فِي طريقي مَاء صافيا وَحَوله عشب من حشيش قد نبت فَقلت فِي نَفسِي يَا سري إِن كنت يَوْمًا أكلت أكله حَلَال وشربت شربة حَلَال فاليوم فَنزلت عَن دَابَّتي فَأكلت من ذَلِك الْحَشِيش وشربت من ذَلِك المَاء فَهَتَفَ بِي هَاتِف سَمِعت الصَّوْت وَلم أر الشَّخْص يَا سري بن الْمُغلس فالنفقة الَّتِي بلغتك إلى هَا هُنَا من أَيْن هِيَ؟ فقصر إِلَيّ نَفسِي.

وَرُوِيَ عَن بَعضهم أنه كَانَ يطْلب الْحَلَال فاستدل عَلَيْهِ فَدلَّ على الْحسن الْبَصْرِيّ بِالْبَصْرَةِ فسافر إليه من بِلَاده الْبَعِيدَة فَقَالَ لَهُ الْحسن إِنَّنِي رجل واعظ آكل من

هَدَايَا النَّاس وضيافاتهم لكنني أدلك على رجل بِبِلَاد سجستان تَرَاهُ فِي مزرعته لَهُ بقرة قد جعل لَهَا فِي أُحْدُ طريقيها تبنا وشعيرا وَفِي الاخر مَاء فَإِذا وصلت الى التِّبْن وَالشعِير عرضهما عَلَيْهَا وَإِذا وصلت إِلى المَاء عرضه عَلَيْهَا فَقَالَ فتوجه الرجل اليه فَوَجَدَهُ كَذَلِك فَسلم عَلَيْهِ وقص عَلَيْهِ حَاله. فَبكى الرجل وَقَالَ قد صدقك الإمام أبو سعيد. لَكِن زَالَ ذَلِك عني بِسَبَب أن الْبَقَرَة عبرت ذَات يَوْم أَرض جاري وَقد اشتغلت عَنْهَا بعلاتي فَعَادَت إِلى أرضي وقوائمها ملطخة بطينها وَاخْتَلَطَ ذَلِك بطين أرضي فَصَارَت شُبْهَة عد إِليه ليدلك على غَيْرِي وَبكى.

وَعَن أبي عبد الله بن الجْلاء قَالَ: أعرف من أقام بِمَكَّة ثَلَاثِينَ سنة لم يشرب من مَاء زَمْزَم غلا مَا استقاه بركوته ورشائه وَلم يتَنَاوَل من طَعَام جلب من مصر شَيْئا.

وَعَن بشر بن الْحَارِث الحافي بن عبد الرَّحْمَن قَالَ سَمِعت الْمعَافى عمرَان يَقُول كَانَ عشرَة فِيمَن مضى من أهل الْعلم ينظرُونَ الْحَلَال الشَّديد لَا يدْخلُونَ بطونهم إِلَّا مَا يعْرفُونَ أَنه من الْحَلَال وَإِلَّا استفوا التُّرَاب ثمَّ عد بشر إِبْرَاهِيم بن أدهم وَسليمَان الْخَواص وَعلي بن فُضَيْل بن عِيَاض وَأَبا مُعَاوِيَة الاسود ويوسف بن أَسْبَاط ووهيب بن الْورْد وَحُذَيْفَة شَيخا من أهل حران وَدَاوُد الطَّائِي وعد بشر عشرَة.

وَعَن يحي بن معِين الْمُحدث:

المَال يذهب حلَّة وحرامة ... يَوْمًا وَتبقى فِي غد آثامه

لَيْسَ التقي بمتق لإلهه ... حَتَّى يطيب شرابه وَطَعَامه

ويطيب مَا تحوي وتكسب كَفه ... وَيكون فِي حسن الحَدِيث كَلَامه

نطق النَّبِي لنا بِهِ عَن ربه ... فعلى النَّبِي صلَاته وَسَلَامه

وَسُئِلَ سُفْيَان الثَّوْرِيّ عَن الْوَرع فَأَنْشد:

إِنِّي وجدت فَلَا تظنوا غَيره ... هَذَا التورع عِنْد هَذَا الدِّرْهَم

فَإِذا قدرت عَلَيْهِ ثمَّ تركته ... فَاعْلَم بِأَن هُنَاكَ تقوى الْمُسلم

وَعَن مُحَمَّد بن عبد الكريم الْمروزِي لما ولي يحي بن أكثم الْقَضَاء كتب اليه اخوه عبد الله بن أكثم من مرو وَكَانَ من الزهاد:

ولقمة بجريش الْملح تأكلها ... الذ من تَمْرَة تحشى بزنبور

وَأكله قربت للهلك صَاحبهَا ... كحبة الفخ دقَّتْ عنق عُصْفُور

وَعَن إِبراهيم بن هشيم أنه استوصاه صَاحب لَهُ عِنْد وداعه فَقَالَ: أوصيك ان يكون عَمَلك صَالحا وتأكل طيبا.

39. The obligation to be scrupulous in matters of food and drink, and to reject what is forbidden

Allāh Taʿālā says: "Forbidden to you are carrion, blood, the meat of pigs, and that over which any name other than Allāh's has been invoked, the animal that has been strangled",[94] and: "Say, I do not find within that which was revealed to me (anything) forbidden to one who would eat it unless it be a dead animal or blood spilled out or the flesh of swine - for indeed, it is impure - or it be (that slaughtered in) disobedience, dedicated to other than Allāh ",[95] "Intoxicants, and games of chance, and idolatrous practices, and the divining of the future are of the loathsome works of the Shaytān; so shun these things",[96] and: "They ask you about intoxicants and games of chance. Say: in both is a major sin",[97] and:

[94] Māida, 3.
[95] Anʿām, 145.
[96] Māida, 90.
[97] Baqara, 219.

"Say: My Lord has forbidden only shameful acts, be they open or secret, and sin, and wrongful oppression",[98] In this verse, ithm (sin) is forbidden explicitly, and it is said that ithm is actually one of the names of wine, as is shown by the following couplet:

I drank ithm, until my mind went awry,
Truly, ithm does away with the minds of men.

It is narrated in the Ṣaḥīḥayn that ʿĀisha رضي الله عنها said that the Rasulullāh ﷺ was once asked about mead (fermented honey and water), and he replied, "Every drink that intoxicates is forbidden."

It is narrated in Ṣaḥīḥ Muslim that Ibn ʿUmar رضي الله عنه that the Prophet ﷺ said, "Every intoxicant is a form of khamr (wine), and all wine is forbidden."

It is narrated in the Ṣaḥīḥayn that Ibn ʿUmar رضي الله عنه that the Prophet ﷺ said "Anyone who drinks wine in this world, and does not then repent, will be forbidden it in the Afterlife."

It is also narrated in the Ṣaḥīḥayn that Abū Hurayra رضي الله عنه said, "During the Isrā (Night Journey), Rasulullāh ﷺ was presented with two cups, one of wine and the other of milk. He looked at them, and chose the milk. And Jibrīl ﷺ said, 'Praised be Allāh, Who has guided you to the Fiṭra.' Had you chosen the wine; your community would have gone astray'."

It is also narrated in the Ṣaḥīḥayn that Abū Hurayra رضي الله عنه said, "When a man drinks wine he is not a believer."

Al-Ḥasan al-Baṣri. said, "How could any man ruin his mind, which is the most beloved thing in Allāh's creation, with wine?"

An Arab was once asked why he did not drink, and he replied, "By Allāh, I am not happy with my mind when it is sound, so why should I corrupt it even further?"

Al-Ḥakam ibn Hisham once said to one of his sons, "O my son! Beware of wine, for it is vomit in your mouth, diarrhoea in your intestines, a ḥadd punishment on your back, and causes children to laugh at you and the Almighty to imprison you."

A wise man once asked his son, "Why do you drink?" and he replied, "It helps with digestion." "By Allāh," his father replied, "it will break up your Dīn even more surely."

[98] Aʿrāf, 33.

ʿAbdullāh ibn Idrīs recited:

Every drink, much of which makes one drunk,
Whether squeezed from dates, or pressed from grapes;
Even a little of it is forbidden,
I warn you: beware of its evil!

Ibn Abil-Dunya heard the following couplet from his father:

If you drink wine, and then more wine on top,
You will damage your Dīn, and empty your purse.

In Ṣaḥīḥ Muslim, and other works, the following ḥadīth is narrated by Abū Hurayra ﷺ that the Prophet ﷺ said "O mankind! Allāh is good, and accepts only that which is good. He has given the believers the command He gave to the Messengers: 'O Messengers! Eat of the good things, and do good also. Truly, I am All-Aware of what you do',[99] and: 'O mankind! Eat of the good things with which We have provided you and be thankful to Allāh, if (indeed) it is Him that you worship.' Then he spoke of a man on a long journey, dishevelled-haired and dusty, who raises his hands up to heaven, saying, 'My Lord! My Lord!' and yet his food is ḥarām, his clothes ḥarām, and his drink ḥarām, and his sustenance ḥarām: how, then, shall his duʿā be answered?"

It is narrated in the Ṣaḥīḥayn that Ibn Bashīr ﷺ that the Prophet ﷺ said, "Ḥalāl is clear and the Ḥarām is clear. But between the two are ambiguous matters not known to many people. Whosoever avoids these matters, has preserved his honour and his Dīn intact. But whosoever falls into them shall fall into the Ḥarām. Similar to a shepherd who grazes his flock around a sanctuary, so that he is near to violating it. Indeed, every king has a sanctuary, and Allāh's sanctuary on this earth is composed of His prohibitions."

It is also narrated in the Ṣaḥīḥayn that Abu Hurayra ﷺ said that the Prophet ﷺ said, "Sometimes when I return to my family, I find a date on my bedding or elsewhere in my house, and raise it to my mouth, but out of fear that it might be from someone's charity, I put it aside."

It is also narrated in Ṣaḥīḥ Bukhari that ʿĀisha رضي الله عنها said that the Abū Bakr ﷺ used to have a servant-boy who would collect the

[99] Mu'minūn, 51.

kharāj for him, and Abū Bakr ﷺ would buy food for himself out of this money. One day, however, the boy brought something, and Abū Bakr ﷺ ate it. 'Do you know what that was?' the boy asked him, and Abū Bakr ﷺ said, 'What was it?' 'In the Jahiliyya', he said, 'I was a soothsayer; something which, in fact, I did not know how to do, but I deceived a man, who met me just now and gave me what you ate.' Abū Bakr ﷺ put his finger into his throat, and vomited all that was in his stomach."

According to Zayd ibn Aslam, 'Umar ibn al-Khattāb ﷺ once drank some milk, which he liked. "Where did you get this milk?" he asked the man who had given it to him, and he replied that he had been on his way to a well, when he passed some animals which had been given in charity, and some people who were milking them; he had taken some of it in his water-skin, and gone away. Hearing this, 'Umar ﷺ put his finger in his throat, and vomited it up.

It is related that 'Āli ﷺ had his bread brought in containers from Madinah.

Yūsuf ibn Asbat said, "When a young man worships, the Shaytān says, 'Look at his food.' If they find his food to be from an impure source, he says: 'Leave him alone; let him worship long and hard, for he himself has ensured that your efforts are not needed.'"

Ḥudhayfa al-Mar'ashi once watched people hurrying to join the first row in a masjid, and said, "They should hurry likewise to eat ḥalāl bread."

When Sufyān al-Thawri was asked about the merit which attaches to praying in the first row, he replied, "Inspect the pieces of bread which you eat, and find out where it comes from, even if this means praying in the last row." He also said, "Look to see where your money comes from, even if you have to pray in the last row."

Sari al-Saqāti used to eat neither the vegetables nor the fruit of southern Iraq, nor anything else which he knew to come from that region. He was very strict in this, by virtue of his great scrupulousness in matters of Dīn. Nevertheless, he said, "Once, when I was at Tarsūs, I was in the company of some young men who were much given to worship. The house contained an oven which they used for baking. When this oven broke, I bought a replacement with my own money, but so great was their scrupulousness that they refused to bake in it."

He once said, "Abū Yūsuf al-Ghasūli used to spend all his time at the war-front, and participate in sorties. When he did so, and he and his companions entered Byzantine territory, the others ate the meat which the Byzantines had slaughtered, while he refrained. "Abū Yūsuf!" he was told, "Do you suspect that it is ḥarām" and he said, "No." "Then eat," they told him, "for it is ḥalāl!" But he remarked, "Renunciation is only of ḥalāl things."

Sari also said, "Returning once from a sortie, I saw by the road some clear water surrounded by some reeds. 'Sari!' I said to myself. 'If you ever eat or drink anything Ḥalāl in your life, then now is the time.' So, I dismounted, and ate and drank, but heard a voice coming from someone I could not see, which said, 'O Sari ibn al-Mughallis! What about the money which enabled you to come here? Where did that come from?' And so, I was disappointed."

ʿAbdullāh ibn al-Jallāʾ said, "I know a man who lived for thirty years in Makkah, who drank the water of Zamzam only when he could use his own bucket and rope, and who never ate any food which had been brought from another town."

Al-Muʿafa ibn ʿImrān said, "In times gone by, there were ten scholars who were particularly careful to ensure that they ate only ḥalāl food. These were: Ibrāhīm ibn Adham, Sulaymān al-Khawwās, ʿAli ibn Fuḍayl, Abū Muʿāwiya al-Aswad, Yūsuf ibn Asbat, Wuhayb ibn al-Ward, Ḥudhayfa of Ḥarān, Dāwūd al-Ṭāī, and two others."

The great Hadīth scholar Yaḥya ibn Maʿīn recited this couplet:

Ḥalāl and ḥarām wealth, both must pass away,
and the sins thereof await the Final Day.

Sufyān al-Thawri was once asked about scrupulousness, and he replied:

I have found, and you must not believe otherwise that scrupulousness applies to every small coin. If you find a coin, but leave it alone, then know that you are a Muslim of piety.

When Yaḥya ibn Aktham was appointed judge, his ascetic brother ʿAbdullāh of Merv wrote to him the following lines:

Many a mouthful with coarse salt which you eat,
is more delicious than a stuffed date.

One bite which destroys a man is like
One seed in a trap, which breaks a bird's neck.

Ibrahīm ibn Hushaim was advised as follows by a friend of his before he left on a journey: "I advise you to act with righteousness, and to eat what is wholesome."

الأربعون من شعب الإيمان

تَحْرِيم الملابس والزّيّ والأواني وَمَا يكره مِنْهَا لحَدِيث أنس بن مَالك فِي الصَّحِيحَيْنِ ((مَنْ لَبِسَ الْحَرِيرَ فِي الدُّنْيَا فَلَنْ يَلْبَسَهُ فِي الأَخِرَةِ)).

وَحَدِيث حُذَيْفَة رَضِي الله عَنهُ ((لَا تَلْبَسُوْا الْحَرِيرَ وَلَا الدِّيْبَاجَ، وَلَا تَشْرَبُوْا فِيْ آنِيَةِ الذَّهَب وَالْفِضَّة، وَلَا تَأْكُلُوا فِي صِحَافِهَا فَإِنَّهَا لَهُم فِي الدُّنْيَا وَهِي لكم فِي الآخِرَة)).

وَحَدِيث إبْن مَسْعُود رَضِي الله عَنهُ فِي صَحِيح مُسلم ((إِن الله جميلٌ يُحِبُّ الْجَمَالَ، الْكِبْرُ بَطَرُ الْحَقِّ وَغَمَطُ النَّاسِ)).

وَحَدِيث أبي بردة رَضِي الله عَنهُ فِي الصَّحِيحَيْنِ قَالَ أَخْرَجَتْ إِلَيْنَا عَائِشَةُ كِسَاءً مُلَبَّدًا وَإِزَارًا غَلِيْظًا فَقَالَتْ قُبِضَ رَسُولُ اللهِ صَلَّى اللهُ عَلَيْهِ وَسلم فِي هذَيْن.

وَحَدِيث عبد الله بن عمر فيهمَا ((لَا يَنْظُرُ اللهُ تَعَالَى يَوْمَ الْقِيَامَةِ إِلَى مَنْ جَرَّ ثَوْبَهُ خُيَلَاءَ)).

40. The prohibition or dislike of certain clothes and eating utensils

It is narrated in the Ṣaḥīḥayn by Anas ibn Mālik ﷺ said that the Prophet ﷺ said, "Whoever wears silk in this world will not wear it in the next."

It is narrated by Ḥudhayfa that the Prophet ﷺ said, "Do not wear

silk, or brocade, and do not eat or drink from vessels of gold or silver, for they are for them in this world, and for you in the next."
It is narrated in the Ṣaḥīḥayn by Ibn Mas'ūd ﷺ said that the Prophet ﷺ said, "Allāh is beautiful, and He loves beauty. Arrogance is to be ungrateful to the True Allāh, and to belittle people."
It is narrated in the Ṣaḥīḥayn that 'Āisha رضي الله عنها once showed us a woollen cloth and a rough waist-wrapper, and said, "Rasulullāh ﷺ passed away wearing these".
It is narrated in the Ṣaḥīḥayn by Ibn 'Umar ﷺ that the Prophet ﷺ said, "On the Day of Reserruction, Allāh Ta'ālā will not look at a man who lets his garment drag on the ground out of pride."

الْحَادِي والاربعون من شعب الإيمان

تَحْرِيم الملاعب والملاهي الْمُخَالفَة للشريعة لقَوْله تَعَالَى ﴿قُل مَا عِنْد اللهِ خَيْرٌ مِنْ اللَّهْوِ وَمِنَ التِّجَارَةِ﴾.

وَلِحَدِيث سُلَيْمَان بن بُرَيْدَة فِي صَحِيح مُسلم عَن أَبيه بُرَيْدَة بن الْحصيب رَضِي الله عَنهُ ((مَنْ لَعِبَ بِالنَّرْدَشِيْرِ فَكَأَنَّمَا صَبَغَ يَدَهُ فِيْ لَحْمِ خِنْزِيْرٍ وَدَمِهِ)).

41. The prohibition of games and amusements which contravene the Shari'a

Allāh Ta'ālā says: "Say, "What is with Allāh is better than playing and than trading".[100]
It is narrated in Ṣaḥīḥ Muslim by Sulaymān ibn Burayda ﷺ that the Prophet ﷺ said, "Whoever plays backgammon has done something akin to dipping his finger into the meat and blood of swine."

[100] Jumu'a, 11.

الثّاني والاربعون من شعب الإيمان

الإقتصاد فِي النَّفَقَة وَتَحْرِيم أكل المَال بِالْبَاطِلِ لقَوْله تَعَالَى ﴿وَلَا تَجْعَلْ يَدَكَ مَغْلُوْلَةً إِلَى عُنُقِكَ وَلَا تَبْسُطْهَا كُلَّ الْبَسْطِ فَتَقْعُدَ مَلُوْمًا مَحْسُوْرًا﴾ وَلقَوْله تَعَالَى ﴿وَالَّذِيْنَ إِذَا أَنْفَقُوْا لَمْ يُسْرِفُوْا وَلَمْ يَقْتُرُوْا وَكَانَ بَيْنَ ذَلِك قَوَامًا﴾.

وَلِحَدِيث الْمُغيرَة بن شُعْبَة رَضِي الله عَنهُ فِي صَحِيح مُسلم وَنهى عَنْ ثَلَاثٍ: قِيْلَ وَقَالٍ، وَإِضَاعَةِ المَالِ، وَكَثْرَةِ السُّؤَالِ.

42. Moderation in expenditure, and the prohibition of consuming wealth unlawfully

Allāh Taʿālā says: "And do not make your hand (as) chained to your neck or extend it completely and (thereby) become blamed and insolvent",[101] and: "And (they are) those who, when they spend, do so not excessively or sparingly but are ever, between that, (justly) moderate".[102]

It is narrated in Ṣaḥīḥ Muslim by Mughīra ibn Shuʿba ﷺ that the Prophet ﷺ mentioned that three things as being forbidden: excessive chitchat, the wasting of money, and excessive asking (others of favours or begging)."

الثّالث والاربعون من شعب الإيمان

ترك الغل والحسد وَنَحْوهمَا لقَوْله تَعَالَى ﴿مِنْ شَرِّ حَاسِدٍ إِذَا حَسَدَ﴾ وَلِقَوْلِهِ تَعَالَى ﴿أَمْ يَحْسُدُوْنَ النَّاسَ عَلَى مَا آتَاهُمُ اللهُ مِنْ فَضْلِهِ﴾.

وَلِحَدِيثِ أَنس رَضِي الله عَنهُ فِي صَحِيح مُسلم ((وَلَا تَحَاسَدُوْا وَلَا تَبَاغَضُوْا وَلَا

[101] Isrā, 29.
[102] Furqān, 67.

تَقَاطَعُوْا وَكُوْنُوْا عِبَادَ اللهِ إِخْوَانًا)).

وَحَدِيث أنس بن مَالك رَضِي الله عَنهُ فِي صَحِيح البُخَارِيّ ((لَا تَبَاغَضُوْا وَلَا تحَاسَدُوْا وَلَا تَدَابِرُوْا وَكُوْنُوْا عِبَادَ اللهِ إِخْوَانًا. وَلَا يحَلُّ لِمُسْلِمٍ أَنْ يَهْجُرَ أَخَاهُ فَوْقَ ثَلَاثِ لَيَالٍ يَلْتَقِيَانِ يَصُدُّ هَذَا وَيَصُدُّ هَذَا، وَخَيْرُهُمَا الَّذِي يَبْدَأُ بِالسَّلَامِ)).

وَبِه أنبأَنَا الْبَيْهَقِيّ بِإِسْنَادِهِ عَن الحسن فِي قَوْله تَعَالَى ﴿وَمِنْ شَرِّ حَاسِدٍ إِذا حَسَدَ﴾ قَالَ هُوَ أَوَّلُ ذَنْبٍ كَانَ فِي السَّمَاء.

وَعَن الأحنف بن قيس خمسٌ هُنَّ كَمَا أقول لَا رَاحَةَ لحسودٍ وَلَا مُرُوءَةَ لَكَذُوْبٍ وَلَا وَفَاءَ لِمُلُوْكٍ وَلَا حِيلَةَ لِبَخِيْل وَلَا سُؤْدُدَ لِسَيِّءِ الخُلُقِ.

وَعَن الخَلِيل بن أَحْمَد مَا رَأَيْتُ ظَالِماً أشبهَ بمظلومٍ من حَاسِدٍ لَهُ نَفَس دَائِم، وعَقْلٌ هَائِمٌ، وَحُزْنٌ لَازمٌ.

وَعَن بِشر بن الحَارِث الحافي الْعَدَاوَةُ فِي الْقَرَابَة والحَسَدُ فِي الجِيرَان وَالْمَنْفَعَةُ فِي الإخوان.

وَعَن المُبَرِّد أنه أنشد:

عينُ الحسُودِ عَلَيْك الدَّهْرَ حارسةٌ ... تُبْدِي المَسَاوِئَ والإحْسَانَ تخْفِيْهِ

يَلقاك بالبِشْر يُبْدِيْهِ مُكَاشَرَةً ... وَالْقَلْبُ مُنْكَتِمُ فِيهِ الَّذِي فِيهِ

إِن الحسودَ بِلَا جُرْمٍ عَدَاوَتُهُ ... وَلَيْسَ يَقْبَلُ عذرًا فِي تجَنِّيْهِ

43. The abandoning of rancour, envy and similar feelings

Allāh Taʿālā says: "And from the evil of the envier when he envies",[103] and: "Or do they envy people for what Allāh has given them of His bounty?"[104]

It is narrated in Ṣaḥīḥ Bukhāri by Anas ﷺ that the Prophet ﷺ said,

---

[103] Falaq, 5.

[104] Nisā, 54.

“Do not hate one another, or envy one another, or turn your backs on one another; rather be Allāh’s slaves while being eachothers brothers. It is not ḥalāl for a Muslim to break off relations with his brother for more than three consecutive nights so that they both turnaway from each other: the better of them is he who gives the first greeting.”
Al-Ḥasan al-Baṣri said in regard to Allāh's statement ‘From the evil of the envier when he envies’, “This was the first sin to have been committed in heaven.”
Al-Aḥnaf ibn Qays said, “Mark these five truths: an envious man finds no peace, a liar has no manly virtue, greedy man is not to be trusted, a a miser has no power, and a man of bad character has no glory.”
Khalīl ibn Aḥmad said, “A man who does wrong through envy is very similar to one who is wronged: he has no peace of mind, and he is always grieved.”
Al-Mubarrid recited the following lines:

The eye of the envier always sees scandal,
Bringing out faults and hiding the good.
He meets you cheerfully, with a smiling face,
while his heart conceals his true feelings.
The envier's enmity comes without. provocation,
yet he accepts no excuses while he attacks.

الرَّابِع والاربعون من شعب الإيمان

تَحْرِيم أعراض النَّاس وَمَا يجب من ترك الوقيعة فِيهَا لقَوْله تَعَالَى ﴿إِنّ الَّذين يُحِبُّوْنَ أَنْ تَشِيْعَ الْفَاحِشَةُ فِي الَّذِيْنَ آمَنُوْا لَهُمْ عَذَابٌ أَلِيْمٌ فِيْ الدُّنْيَا وَالآخِرَة﴾ وَقوله تَعَالَى ﴿إِنّ الَّذِيْنَ يَرْمُوْنَ الْمُحْصَنَاتِ الْغَافِلَاتِ الْمُؤْمِنَاتِ لُعِنُوْا فِي الدُّنْيَا والآخِرَةِ﴾ وَغير ذَلِك من الآيات والأخبار الْكَثِيرَة.
وكحديث أَبي هُرَيْرَة فِي صَحِيح مُسلم ((الْمُسلمُ أَخُو الْمُسْلِمِ لَا يُسْلِمُهُ وَلَا يَخْذُلُهُ وَلَا يَحْقِرُهُ، التَّقْوَى هَا هُنَا)) وَيُشِير إِلَى صَدْرِهِ ثَلَاثَ مَرَّاتٍ ((بِحَسْبِ امْرِئٍ مِنَ الشَّرِّ

أن يَحْقِرَ أَخَاهُ الْمُسْلِمَ. كُلُّ الْمُسْلِمِ عَلَى الْمُسْلِمِ حَرَامٌ: دَمُهُ وَمَالُهُ وَعِرْضُهُ)).

وَحَدِيث أبي ذَرٍّ رَضِي الله عَنهُ فِي الصَّحِيح ((لَا يَرْمِي رَجُلٌ رَجلاً بِالْفِسْقِ وَلَا يَرْمِيْهِ بِالْكُفْرِ إِلَّا ارْتَدَّتْ عَلَيْهِ إِن لَمْ يَكُنْ صَاحِبُهُ كَذَلِك)).

44. The sanctity of people's reputations, and the obligation not to cast aspersions upon them

Allāh Taʿālā says: "Indeed, those who like that immorality should be spread (or publicised) among those who have believed will have a painful punishment in this world and the Hereafter",[105] and: "Verily, those who accuse chaste women, who never even think of anything touching their chastity and are good believers, are cursed in this life and in the Hereafter".[106] There are many other verses which deal with the same subject.

It is narrated in Ṣaḥīḥ Muslim by Abu Hurayra ﵁ that the Prophet ﷺ said: "Every Muslim is a brother to every other Muslim; he neither disparages, humiliates, or despises him. The fear of Allāh lies here," and he pointed to his heart three times. "It is sufficient evil for a man that he despises his brother Muslim. A Muslim is entirely sacrosanct to every other Muslim: his blood, his possessions and his honour."

It is narrated in Ṣaḥīḥ Bukhāri by Abu Dharr ﵁ that the Prophet ﷺ said, "Let no man accuse another of unrighteousness or kufr, lest, should he be mistaken and he himself be as he says."

الْخَامِس والاربعون من شعب الإيمان

إخلاص الْعَمَل لله عزوجل وَترك الرِّيَاء وَلقَوْله تَعَالَى ﴿وَمَا أُمِرُوْا إِلَّا لِيَعْبُدُوْا اللهَ مُخْلِصِيْنَ لَهُ الدّين حُنَفَاءَ﴾ وَقَوله تَعَالَى ﴿مَنْ كَانَ يُرِيْدُ حَرْث الآخِرَةِ نَزِدْ لَهُ فِي

[105] Nūr, 19.
[106] Nūr, 23.

حَرْثِهِ وَمَنْ كَانَ يُرِيدُ حَرْثَ الدُّنْيَا نُؤْتِهِ مِنْهَا وَمَا لَهُ فِي الْآخِرَةِ مِنْ نَصِيبٍ﴾ وَقوله تَعَالَى ﴿مَنْ كَانَ يُرِيدُ الْحَيَاةَ الدُّنْيَا وَزِينَتَهَا نُوَفِّ إِلَيْهِمْ أَعْمَالَهُمْ فِيهَا وَهُمْ فِيهَا لَا يُبْخَسُونَ أُولَئِكَ الَّذِينَ لَيْسَ لَهُمْ فِي الْآخِرَةِ إِلَّا النَّارُ وَحَبِطَ مَا صَنَعُوا فِيهَا وَبَاطِلٌ مَا كَانُوا يعْمَلُونَ﴾ وَقوله تَعَالَى ﴿فَمَنْ كَانَ يَرْجُو لِقَاءَ رَبِّهِ فَلْيَعْمَلْ عَمَلًا صَالِحًا وَلَا يُشْرِكْ بِعِبَادَةِ رَبِّهِ أَحَدًا﴾.

وَالحَدِيث أبي هُرَيْرَة رَضِي الله عَنهُ فِي صَحِيح مُسلم ((قَالَ اللهُ عَزّ وَجلّ أَنَا أَغْنَى الشُّرَكَاءِ عَنِ الشِّرْكِ فَمَنْ عَمِلَ لِيْ عَمَلًا أَشْرَكَ فِيْهِ مَعِيْ غَيْرِيْ فَأَنَا مِنْهُ بَرِيْءٌ وَهُوَ لِلَّذِيْ أَشْرَكَ)).

وَالحَدِيث جُنْدُب رَضِي الله عَنهُ فِي الصَّحِيحَيْنِ ((مَنْ سَمَّعَ سَمَّعَ اللهُ بِهِ وَمَنْ يُرَائِيْ يُرَائِي اللهُ بِهِ)).

أنبأني الْبَيْهَقِيّ بِإِسْنَادِهِ إن أبا حَمْزَة سُئِلَ عَن الإخلاص. فَقَالَ مَا لَا يُحِبُّ أَنْ يَحْمَدَهُ عَلَيْهِ إلاَّ الله عزّ وَجلّ. وَعَن سهل بن عبد الله لَا يَعْرِفُ الرِّيَاءَ إلاّ مُخْلِصٌ وَلَا النِّفَاق إلا مُؤمنٌ وَلَا الْجَهْل إلا عَالِمٌ وَلَا الْمَعْصِيَةَ إلا مُطِيْعٌ. وَعَنِ الرّبيعِ بن خُثَيْم كُلُّ مَا لَا يُبْتَغِي بِهِ وَجْهَ اللهِ يَضْمَحِلُّ. وَعَن الْجُنَيْدِ لَوْ أَنَّ عَبْدًا أَتَى بافتقار آدم وزهد عِيسَى وَجُهْدِ أيوبَ وَطَاعَة يحي وإستقامة إدريس وود الْخَلِيل وَخُلُقِ الحبيبِ وَكَانَ فِي قلبه ذَرَّةٌ لِغَيْرِ اللهِ فَلَيْسَ لِلّهِ فِيهِ حَاجَةٌ. وَعَنْ زُبَيْدٍ بن الْحَارِث اليامي يَسُرُّنِيْ أنْ يَكُوْنَ لِيْ فِيْ كُلِّ شَيْءٍ نِيَّةٌ حَتَّى فِي الأكلِ وَالشربِ وَالنَّوْم. وَعَن سُفْيَان ﴿كُلُّ شَيْءٍ هَالِكٌ إلاَّ وَجْهَهُ﴾. قَالَ مَا أريدَ بِهِ وَجْهُه. وَعَن هِلَال بن يسَاف قَالَ عِيسَى بن مَرْيَم صلوَات الله عَلَيْهِ إذا كَانَ يَوْمُ صَوْم أحدكم فليدهن لحيته وليمسح شَفَتَيْه وَيخرج إِلَى النَّاس حَتَّى كَأَنَّهُ لَيْسَ بصائم وإذا أعطى بِيَمِينِهِ فَلْيُخْفِهِ عَن شِمَاله وإذا صلَّى أحدكم فلْيُسْدِلْ سِتْرَ بَابه فَإِن الله تَعَالَى يقسم

الثَّناء كَمَا يقسم الرِّزْق. وَعَن ذِي النُّون الْمصْرِيّ قَالَ بعض الْعلمَاء مَا أخلص الْعَبْد لله إلا أحبَّ أن يكون فِي جُبٍّ لَا يُعْرَف. وَعَن بشر بن الْحَارِث عَن الفُضَيْل بن عِيَاض لَأن آكل الدُّنْيَا بالطَّبَلِ والمِزْمَارِ أحبُّ إلَيّ من أن آكُلَهَا بِدِيْنٍ. وَعَن مَالك بن أنس قَالَ لي أستاذي ربيعَة الرَّأْي يَا مَالِكُ مَنْ السَّفَلَةُ؟ قلتُ مَنْ أَكَلَ بِدِينِهِ. فَقَالَ مَنْ سَفَلَةُ السَّفَلَةِ. قَالَ مَنْ أَصْلَحَ دنيا غَيره بِفساد دينه قَالَ فصدَّقَني.

وَعَن إبْن الأعرابي أخسرُ الخاسرين من أبدى للنَّاس صَالحَ أعماله وبارز بالقبيح مَنْ هُوَ أقْربُ إليه مِن حَبْل الوريد. وَعَن سُفْيَان: يَا معشر الْقُرَّاء إرْفَعُوا رؤوسَكم، لَا تَزِيدُوا الْخُشُوعَ على مَا فِي الْقلب، فقد وَضَحَ الطَّرِيق، فَاتَّقُوا اللهَ، وأَجْمِلُوْا فِي الطَّلَبِ وَلَا تَكُونُوا عِيَالًا على الْمُسلمين. وَعَن بعض الْعلمَاء خوِّفوا الْمُؤمنِينَ بِاللهِ، وَالْمُنَافِقِينَ بالسلطان، والمُرَائِيْنَ بِالنَّاسِ.

45. Ikhlās (sincerety), so that one acts only for Allāh Taʿālā, and avoids all forms of riyā (ostentation)

Allāh Taʿālā says: "They were only commanded to worship Allāh, sincere in their Dīn to Him, and to be those inclining to the the truth",[107] and: "Whoever desires the harvest of the Hereafter - We increase for him in his harvest. And whoever desires the harvest of this world - We give him thereof, but there is not for him in the Hereafter any share,",[108] and: "Whoever desires the life of this world and its adornments - We fully repay them for their deeds therein, and they therein will not be deprived. Those are the ones for whom there is not in the Hereafter but the Fire. And lost is what they did therein, and worthless is what they used to do",[109] and:

[107] Bayyina, 5.
[108] Shurā, 20.
[109] Hūd, 15-16.

"So whoever would hope for the meeting with his Lord - let him do righteous work and not associate in the worship of his Lord anyone." [110]

It is narrated in Ṣaḥīḥ Muslim by Abu Hurayra ﵁ that the Prophet ﷺ said: "Allāh ﷻ says: 'I am in less need of partners than anyone else. Therefore, when a man does anything for My sake, and for the sake of another as well, then I absolve myself of him, and he is left to what he took as a partner to Me'."

It is narrated in the Ṣaḥīḥayn by Jundub ﵁ that the Prophet ﷺ said, "Whoever acts to be heard and seen, Allāh will cause his falsity to be heard and seen."

Abū ʿUmar was once asked about sincerity, and replied, "It is present when one wishes to be praised for something only by Allāh."

Sahl ibn ʿAbdullāh said, "Only a sincere person knows about riyā (showing-off); only a believer knows about hypocrisy; only a man of learning knows about ignorance; and only a man who obeys Allāh knows what it is to disobey Him."

Al-Rabīʿ ibn Khuthaym said, "Every act which is not performed for the sake of Allāh comes to naught."

Al-Junayd said, "Even if a man were as poor as Ādam, as ascetic as ʿĪsā, as prone to trials as Ayyūb, as obedient as Yaḥya, as upright as Idrīs, as loving as Ibrāhīm عَلَيْهِمُ السَّلَامُ, and as superb in character as Muḥammed ﷺ, and yet harboured in his heart an iota of desire for other than Allāh, then Allāh would have no need of him."

Zubayd said, "It pleases me to make an intention before doing anything at all, even if it be eating, drinking and going to sleep."

Sufyān said in connection with the verse "Everything shall perish except His countenance",[111] that it can be interpreted as meaning, "Everything that is not done for His sake shall perish."

ʿĪsā son of Maryam عَلَيْهِ السَّلَامُ said, "When a man fasts, he should put some oil on his beard and wipe his lips, and go out before people as though he were not fasting. When he gives something with his right hand, he should hide it from his left. When a man prays, he

---

[110] Kahf, 110.

[111] Qaṣaṣ, 88.

should hang down the curtain of his door."
According to Dhun-Nūn, one of the ʿulamā said, "Whenever a man does something sincerely for Allāh, he feels a longing to be in a cave where he will not be recognised."
Al-Fuḍayl ibn Īyāḍ said, "I would prefer to acquire the things of this world by playing drums and flutes than to do so with the things of Dīn."
Imām Mālik ibn Anas رَحِمَهُ ٱللَّهُ said, "My teacher, Rabīʿa al-Ray, once asked me, 'O Mālik, who is the lowest of men?' and I replied, 'He who uses Dīn to acquire worldly things.' 'And who is lower than that?' he asked, and I answered, 'He who improves the worldly condition of others by damaging his Dīn.' And he told me that I was correct."
Ibn al-ʿArabi رَحِمَهُ ٱللَّهُ said, "The greatest of all losers is the one who shows his good deeds to other people, but his sins defy the One Who is closer to him than his jugular vein."
Sufyān said, "O reciters of the Qurʾān! Raise your heads, for there can be no greater humility than that which is concealed in the heart. The way is well-known; therefore, fear Allāh, and seek your own sustenance, and do not be dependant on Muslim charity."
One of the ʿulamā said, "Put the fear of Allāh into the hearts of the believers, and the fear of the ruler into the hearts of the hypocrites, and the fear of other people into the hearts of those who show off."

السَّادِس والاربعون من شعب الإيمان

السرُور بِالْحَسَنَة والاغتمام بِالسَّيِّئَة لحَدِيث جَابر بن سَمُرَة عَن عمر بن الْخطاب رَضِي الله عَنهُ فِي سنَن أبي دَاوُد ((وَمن سرّته حسنته وساءته سيئته فَهُوَ مُؤمن)).

46. Happiness when one has done a good deed, and sorrow when one has commited a sin

It is narrated by Abū Dāwūd that ʿUmar ibn al-Khattāb رَضِيَ ٱللَّهُ عَنْهُ quoted the ḥadīth: "Whoever is made happy by his good deed, and sorrowful by commiting sin, is a believer."

السَّابع والأربعون من شعب الإيمان

معالجة كل ذَنْب بِالتَّوْبَةِ لقَوْله تَعَالَى ﴿وتوبوا إلى الله جَمِيعًا أَيها الْمُؤْمِنُونَ لَعَلَّكُمْ تفلحون﴾ وَقَوله تَعَالَى ﴿تُوبُوا إلى الله تَوْبَة نصُوحًا﴾ وَقَوله تَعَالَى ﴿وأنيبوا إلى ربكُم وأَسْلِمُوْا لَهُ﴾.

وَلِحَدِيث أبي بردة بن أبي مُوسَى الأشعريّ عَن الأغر الْمُزنِيّ فِي صَحِيح مُسلم وَسنَن أبي دَاوُد وَغَيرهمَا ((إنّه لَيُغَانُ عَلَى قلبِي وإنِّي لَأَسْتَغْفِرُ اللهَ فِي الْيَوْمِ مِئَة مَرَّةٍ)).

47. Treating every sin with repentance

Allāh Taʿālā says: Turn to Allāh in repentance, all you believers, that you might succeed",[112] and: "O you who have believed, repent to Allāh with sincere repentance",[113] and: "Return [in repentance] to your Lord and submit to Him".[114]

It is narrated in Ṣaḥīḥ Muslim by al-Aʿaz al-Muzani ﷺ that the Prophet ﷺ said: "My heart is sometimes clouded[115] and I ask for Allāh's forgiveness a hundred times each day."

---

[112] Nūr, 31.

[113] Tahrim, 8.

[114] Zumar, 54.

[115] When the Prophet ﷺ is referring to his heart becoming clouded, he does not mean the heart becoming sullied or rusted due to excess negligence and sins, like the average person. Imām Nawawi رحمه الله in his commentary of Ṣaḥīḥ Muslim has mentioned many views of what this means. One view is that when the Prophet ﷺ became deeply engrossed in the matters of the umma such as its defence from enemies and upon attending to those matters, he would then re-engage with direct worship at his own lofty spiritual station before his Lord with istighfār. While another view is that the cloud on his heart meant a special sakīnah descending upon him and as thankfulness to his Lord, he engaged in istighfār.

الثَّامِن وَالأربعون من شعب الإيمان

الْقَرَابِينَ وجملتها الْهَدْي والأضحية والعقيقة لقوله تَعَالَى ﴿فَصَلِّ لِرَبِّكَ وَانْحَرْ﴾ وَقوله تَعَالَى ﴿وَالْبُدْنَ جَعَلْنَاهَا لَكُم مِّن شَعَائِرِ اللَّهِ لَكُمْ فِيهَا خَيْرٌ﴾ وَقوله تَعَالَى ﴿وَمَن يُعَظِّمْ شَعَائِرَ اللَّهِ فَإِنَّهَا مِن تَقْوَى الْقُلُوبِ﴾ الآيَات. وَلِحَدِيث أَنس بن مَالك رَضِي الله عَنهُ فِي الصَّحِيحَيْنِ أَن رَسُول الله صلى الله عَلَيْهِ وَسلم كَانَ يُضَحِّي بِكَبْشَيْنِ أقرنين أملحين وَلَقَد رَأَيْتُهُ يضع رجله فِي صِفَاحِهِمَا وَيُسَمِّي وَيُكَبِّرُ وَفِي رِوَايَة وَلَقَد رَأَيْته يذبحهما بِيَدِهِ.

48. Sacrifices, namely hady (hajj-related sacrifice), and the sacrifices for the ʿĪd and for Aqiqa

Allāh Taʿālā says: "So pray to your Lord and sacrifice",[116] and: "And the camels and cattle We have appointed for you as among the symbols of Allāh; for you therein is good".[117] And: "Whoever honors the symbols of Allāh, indeed, it is from the piety of hearts."[118]

It is narrated in the Ṣaḥīḥayn by Anas bin Mālik ﷺ said that "the Prophet ﷺ used to offer a sacrifice of two white rams with horns. I saw him sacrificing them by placing his leg upon their sides and saying, 'Bismillāh' and 'Allāhu Akbar'. In another narration it is said that he slaughtered them with his own hands."

التَّاسِعُ وَالْأَرْبَعُونَ من شعب الإيمان

طَاعَةُ الْأَمْرِ لقَوْله تَعَالَى ﴿أَطِيعُوا اللَّهَ وَأَطِيعُوا الرَّسُولَ وَأُولِي الأَمْرِ مِنْكُمْ﴾ قيل

---

[116] Kawthar, 2.
[117] Hajj, 36.
[118] Hajj, 32.

هم أمراء السَّرَايَا وَقيل هم الْعلمَاء وَيحْتَمل أن يكون عَامًّا لَهما فَإِن كَانَ خَاصًّا فبأمر السَّرَايَا أشبه.
وَلِحَدِيث أبي هُرَيْرَة فِي الصَّحِيحَيْنِ ((من أطاعني فقد أطاع الله وَمن عَصَانِي فقد عصى الله وَمن يطع الأمير فقد أطاعني وَمن يعْص الأمير فقد عَصَانِي)).
وَلِحَدِيث أبي ذَر فيهمَا يَا أبا ذَر ((إسْمَع وأطع وَلَو عبدا حَبَشِيًّا مُجَدَّعَ الأطرَافِ)).

49. Obedience to those in authority.

Allāh Taʿālā says: "Obey Allāh, and His Messenger, and those in authority among you".[119] It is said that this refers to men in authority over an army detachment, or to the ʿulama. Although the former application is more probable, it may apply to both.
It is narrated in the Ṣaḥīḥayn by Abu Hurayra ﷺ that the Prophet ﷺ said, "Whoever obeys me has obeyed Allāh, and whoever disobeys me has disobeyed Allāh. Whoever obeys the commander, has obeyed me, and whoever disobeys him, has disobeyed me."
They also narrate from Abū Dharr ﷺ that the Prophet ﷺ said, "Abū Dharr! Hear and obey, even if it be to a limbless Abyssinian slave."

الْخَمْسُونَ من شعب الإيمان

التَّمَسُّك بِمَا عَلَيْهِ الْجَمَاعَة لقَوْله تَعَالَى ﴿واعتصموا بِحَبل الله جَمِيعًا وَلَا تفرقُوا﴾. وَلِحَدِيث أبي هُرَيْرَة فِي صَحِيح مُسلم ((من خرج من الطَّاعَة وَفَارق الْجَمَاعَة ثمَّ مَاتَ مَاتَ ميتَة جَاهِلِيَّة)).
وَحَدِيث عرْفجَة بن شُرَيْح الاشجعي رَضِي الله عَنهُ فِي صَحِيح مُسلم ايضا ((سَتَكُون بعدِي هَنَات وهنات فَمن رَأَيْتُمُوهُ يفرق أَمر أمة مُحَمَّد وَهِي جَمِيع

[119] Nisā, 59.

فَاقْتُلُوهُ كَائِنًا مَن كَانَ مِنَ النَّاسِ)).

50. Holding firmly to the Jamāʿa[120]

Allāh Taʿālā says: "And hold firmly to the rope of Allāh all together and do not become divided".[121]
It is narrated in Ṣaḥīḥ Muslim by Abū Hurayra ؓ that the Prophet ﷺ said, "Whoever is disobedient, and departs from the Jamāʿa, and then dies, has died in a state of Jāhiliyya".
It is also narrated in Ṣaḥīḥ Muslim by ʿArfaja Ibn Shurayḥ AL-Ashjaʿī ؓ "After I am gone, there will come days of corruption and turmoil. When you see people dividing the unity of the umma of Muḥammed, you must kill them, whoever they may happen to be."

الحَادِي وَالخَمْسُونَ من شعب الإيمان

الحكم بَين النَّاس بِالْعَدْلِ لقَوْله تَعَالَى ﴿وَإِذَا حَكَمْتُم بَيْنَ النَّاسِ أَن تَحْكُمُوا بِالْعَدْلِ﴾ وَقَوْلُهُ تَعَالَى ﴿وَلَا تَكُنْ لِلْخَائِنِينَ خَصِيمًا﴾ وَقوله تَعَالَى ﴿وَأَقسطوا إِن الله يحب المقسطين﴾ الْآيَات.

وَلِحَدِيث عبد الله إبن مَسْعُود رَضِي الله عَنهُ فِي الصَّحِيحَيْنِ ((لَا حسد إلا فِي اثْنَتَيْنِ رجل آتَاهُ الله مَالا فَسَلَّطَهُ على هَلَكته فِي الْحق وَآخر آتَاهُ الله حِكْمَةً فَهُوَ يقْضِي بهَا وَيُعَلِّمُهَا)).

---

[120] "The order to stick to the Jamāʿa means sticking to the Haq and it's followers; even if those who stick to the truth are a minority and those who oppose it are the majority.
[121] Āl ʿImrān, 103.

51. Passing judgement between people with justice

Allāh Taʿālā says: "And when you judge between people, judge with justice",[122] and: "And do not be for the deceitful an advocate",[123] and: "Act justly. Indeed, Allāh loves those who act justly".[124]
It is narrated in the Ṣaḥīḥayn by Ibn Masʿūd ﷺ that the Prophet ﷺ said "Only two men may be envied: a man whom Allāh has given wealth, and he uses it by spending it in ways which please Him, and a man whom Allāh has given wisdom, and he judges in accordance with it, and teaches it to others."

الثَّانِي وَالْخَمْسُونَ من شعب الإيمان

الأمر بِالْمَعْرُوفِ وَالنَّهْي عَنِ الْمُنكر لقَوْله تَعَالَى ﴿وَلْتَكُن مِّنكُمْ أُمَّةٌ يَدْعُوْنَ إلى الْخَيْر ويأمرون بِالْمَعْرُوفِ وَينْهَوْنَ عَن الْمُنكر وَأُولَئِكَ هم المفلحون﴾ وَقَوله تَعَالَى ﴿كُنْتُم خيرَ أمة أُخْرِجَتْ لِلنَّاسِ تَأْمُرُوْنَ بِالْمَعْرُوفِ وَتَنْهَوْنَ عَنِ الْمُنْكَرِ وَتُؤْمِنُوْنَ بِاللهِ﴾ وَقَوله تَعَالَى ﴿إن الله اشْترى من الْمُؤمنِينَ أنفسهم وأموالهم بِأَنَّ لَهُمُ الْجَنَّةَ﴾ إلى قَوْلِهِ ﴿الآمِرُوْنَ بِالْمَعْرُوفِ والنَّاهُوْنَ عَنِ الْمُنْكَرِ﴾ الْآيَات وَقَوله تَعَالَى ﴿لُعِنَ الَّذين كَفَرُوْا مِنْ بَنِيْ إِسْرَائِيْلَ عَلَى لِسَانِ دَاوُدَ وَعِيسَى بْنِ مَرْيَمَ ذَلِكَ بِمَا عَصَوْا وَكَانُوْا يَعْتَدُوْنَ كَانُوْا لَا يَتَنَاهُوْنَ عَنِ مُنْكَرٍ فَعَلُوْهُ لَبِئْسَ مَا كَانُوا يَفْعَلُونَ﴾ وَالْقرَان مشحون بهما.

وَالْحَدِيث أبي سعيد رَضِي الله عَنهُ فِي صَحِيح مُسلم ((من رأى مِنْكُم مُنْكَرًا فَلْيُغَيِّرْهُ بِيَدِهِ فَإِن لَمْ يَسْتَطِعْ فَبِلِسَانِهِ فَإِنْ لَمْ يَسْتَطِعْ فَبِقَلْبِهِ وَذَلِكَ أَضْعَفُ الْإِيْمَانِ)) وَحَدِيث عبد الله بنِ مَسْعُودٍ رَضِي الله عَنهُ فِيهِ أيضا ((مَا من نَبِيٍّ بَعَثَهُ

---

[122] Nisā, 58.
[123] Nisā, 105.
[124] Ḥujurāt, 9.

اللهُ فِي أُمَّتِهِ قَبْلِي إِلا كَانَ لَهُ فِي أمته حواريون وأصحاب يَأْخُذُونَ بسنته ويَقْتَدُوْنَ بِأَمْرِهِ ثُمَّ إِنَّهَا تَخْلُفُ مِنْ بعدهِمْ خُلُوْفٌ يَقُوْلُوْنَ مَا لَا يَفْعَلُونَ وَيَفْعَلُوْنَ مَا لَا يُؤْمَرُوْنَ فَمَنْ جَاهَدَهُمْ بِيَدِهِ فَهُوَ مُؤمِنٌ وَمَنْ جَاهَدَهُمْ بِلِسَانِهِ فَهُوَ مُؤمِنٌ وَمَنْ جَاهَدَهُمْ بِقَلْبِهِ فَهُوَ مُؤمِنٌ وَلَيْسَ وَرَاءَ ذَلِك من الإيمان حَبَّة خَرْدَل)) وَ فِي الصَّحِيحَيْنِ من حَدِيث سُفْيَان بن عُيَيْنَة عَن الزُّهْرِيّ عَن عُرْوَة عَن زَيْنَب بنت أبي سَلمَة عَن حَبِيبَة عَن أمها أم حَبِيبَة عَن زَيْنَب زوج النَّبِي صلى الله عَلَيْهِ وَسلم قَالَت إِسْتَيْقَظَ النَّبِي صلى الله عَلَيْهِ وَسلم مِنْ نومٍ مُحْمَرًّا وَجْهُهُ وَهُوَ يَقُول ((لَا اله الا الله ثَلَاث مَرَّات ويلٌ للْعَرَب من شَرّ قد اقْتَرَبَ فُتِحَ الْيَوْمَ مِنْ رَدْمِ يَأْجُوجَ وَمَأْجُوجَ مِثْلُ هَذِهِ)) وَحلّق حلقة بِأُصْبُعَيْهِ الإبهام وَالَّتِي تَلِيهَا قَالَت زَيْنَب فَقلت ((يَا رَسُولَ الله أ نُهْلِك وَفينَا الصالحون؟)) قَالَ ((نعم إِذا كَثُرَ الْخَبَثُ)) وَبه أَنبأَنَا الْبَيْهَقِيّ بِإِسْنَادِهِ عَن مَالك بن دِينَار أنه قرا هَذِه الْآيَة ﴿وَكَانَ فِي الْمَدِينَةِ تِسْعَةُ رَهْطٍ يُفْسِدُوْنَ فِي الْأَرْضِ وَلَا يُصْلِحُوْنَ﴾ فَأَما الْيَوْم فَفِي كل قَبيلَة وَحيّ من الَّذين يفسدون فِي الأرض وَلَا يصلحون.

وَعنهُ أيضا ((أن الله عز وَجل أمْر بقرية أن تعذّب فضجّت الْمَلَائِكَة)) وَقَالَت ((إِن فيهم عَبدك فلَانا﴾ قَالَ ((أسمعوني مِنْهُ صَيْحَة فَإِن وَجهه لم يتمعّر غَضبًا لمحارمي)) وَرُوِيَ ذَلِك مَرْفُوعا إِلَى النَّبِي صلى الله عَلَيْهِ وَسلم بِإِسْنَاد ضَعِيف وَعنهُ أيضا ((اصطلحنا على حب الدُّنْيَا فلَا يَأْمر بَعْضنَا بَعْضًا وَلَا يُنْهِي بَعْضنَا بَعْضًا وَلَا يذرنا الله تَعَالَى على هَذَا فليت شعري أَي عَذَاب ينزل)) وَعَن عمر بن عبد الْعَزِيز قَالَ ((كَانَ يُقَال إِن الله عز وَجل لَا يعذّب الْعَامَّة بذنب الْخَاصَّة وَلَكِن اذا عُمل الْمُنكر جهارًا فَلم ينكروه استحقوا الْعقُوبَة كلهم)).

52. Enjoining good, and forbidding evil

Allāh Taʿālā says: "And let there be [arising] from you a nation inviting to [all that is] good, enjoining what is right and forbidding what is wrong, and those will be the successful",[125] and: "You are the best nation produced [as an example] for mankind. You enjoin what is right and forbid what is wrong and believe in Allāh,"[126] and: "[Such believers are] the repentant, the worshippers, the praisers [of Allāh], the travelers [for His cause], those who bow and prostrate [in prayer], those who enjoin what is right and forbid what is wrong",[127] and: "Cursed were those who disbelieved among the Children of Israel by the tongue of David and of Jesus, the son of Mary. That was because they disobeyed and [habitually] transgressed. They used not to prevent one another from wrongdoing that they did. How wretched was that which they were doing".[128] The Qurʾān is full of such verses.
It is narrated in Ṣaḥīḥ Muslim by Abū Saʿīd al-Khudri رضي الله عنه that the Prophet ﷺ said, "Whoever sees something evil should change it with his hand. If he cannot, then with his tongue; and if he cannot do even that, then in his heart. That is the weakest degree of faith."
It is also narrated in Ṣaḥīḥ Muslim by Ibn Masʿūd رضي الله عنه that the Prophet ﷺ said, "There was not a single Prophet among those who were sent before me who did not have disciples and companions who followed his Sunna and obeyed his commands. But afterwards other generations came whose words belied their deeds, and whose deeds were not in accordance with what they commanded others to do. Whoever struggles against them with his hand is a believer. Whoever struggles against them with his tongue is a believer. And whoever struggles against them with his heart is a believer. But when none of these things are done, then not a single mustard seed's weight of faith is present."
It is narrated in the Ṣaḥīḥayn by Zaynab رضي الله عنها, the wife of the

[125] Āl ʿImrān, 104.
[126] Āl ʿImrān, 110.
[127] Tawba, 112.
[128] Māida, 79.

Prophet ﷺ said, "The Prophet ﷺ once awoke, and his face was dark, as he said three times, 'There is no one worthy of worship except Allāh! Woe to the Arabs, because of an evil which will soon come! Today, the barrier of Yaʾjūj and Maʾjūj has been breached by so much,' and he made a circle with his thumb and forefinger. And Zaynab رضي الله عنها remarked, "I said, 'O Rasulullāh! Even when the righteous still dwell among us?' and he said, 'Yes, when corruption becomes widespread'."

Mālik ibn Dinār once recited the verse: "And there were in the city nine family heads causing corruption in the land and not amending [its affairs]",[129] and said, "Nowadays, there are people in every clan and district who cause corruption in the earth, and do not cause reform."

He also said, "We have become accustomed to loving the world, so that we do not enjoin good or forbid evil to one another. Allāh Taʿālā will certainly not permit us to continue doing this, but would that I knew what kind of punishment shall befall us!"

ʿUmar ibn ʿAbdul ʿAzīz said, "It used to be said that Allāh Taʿālā does not punish the common people for the sins of the elite; but when evil is done openly, and they do not repudiate it, they all become deserving of His punishment."

الثَّالِث وَالْخَمْسُونَ من شعب الإيمان

التعاون على الْبر وَالتَّقْوى لقَوْله تَعَالَى ﴿وَتَعَاوَنُوْا عَلَى البِرِّ وَالتَّقوَى وَلَا تَعَاوَنُوْا عَلَى الإِثْمِ والْعُدْوَانِ﴾.

وَلِحَدِيث أنس بن مَالك رَضِي الله عَنهُ فِي الصَّحِيحَيْنِ ((أُنْصُرْ أخاك ظَالِما أَوْ مَظْلُوما)) فَقَالَ رجل ((يَا رَسُول الله أَنْصُرُهُ مَظْلُوما فَكيف أنصره ظَالِما)) فَقَالَ ((تَمنعهُ من الظُّلم فَذَلِك نَصْرُك إياه)).

[129] Naml, 48.

53. Cooperation in goodness and piety

Allāh Taʿālā says: "And cooperate in righteousness and piety, but do not cooperate in sin and aggression".[130]
It is also narrated in the Ṣaḥīḥayn by Anas ibn Mālik ﷺ that the Prophet ﷺ said "Help your brother, whether he is wronged or doing wrong." A man said, "O Rasulullāh! I can help him when he is wronged, but how may I help him when he is doing wrong?" And he replied, "By preventing him from doing it; thus, can you be of help to him."

الرَّابِع وَالْخَمْسُونَ من شعب الإيمان

الْحَيَاءُ لحَدِيث سَالم بن عبد الله بن عمر رَضِي الله عَنْهُمَا فِي الصَّحِيحَيْنِ عَن أَبِيه عَن النَّبِي صلى الله عَلَيْهِ وَسلم أنه سمع رجلا يعظ أخاه فِي الْحَيَاء فَقَالَ ((دَعْهُ فَإِنَّ الْحَيَاءَ مِنَ الْإِيْمَانِ)) وَلحَدِيث عِمرَان بن حُصَيْن رَضِي الله عَنهُ فيهمَا ((إِن الْحَيَاءَ لَا يَأْتِيْ إلا بِخَير)) وَلحَدِيث أبي سعيد الْخُدْرِيّ رَضِي الله عَنهُ فيهمَا أيضا قَالَ كَانَ رَسُول الله صلى الله عَلَيْهِ وَسلم أشد حَيَاءً من الْعَذْرَاء فِي خِدْرِهَا وَكَانَ إِذا كَرِهَ شَيْئًا عَرفْنَاهُ فِي وَجْهِهِ وَحَدِيث أبي مَسْعُود الأنصاري رَضِي الله عَنهُ فِي صَحِيح البُخَارِيّ ((إِن مِمَّا أَدْرَكَ النَّاسُ مِنْ كَلَامِ النُّبُوَّةِ الأُوْلَى إذا لَمْ تَسْتَحِ فَاصْنَعْ مَا شِئْتَ)).

54. Modesty

It is narrated in the Ṣaḥīḥayn by Ibn ʿUmar ﷺ that the Prophet ﷺ once heard a man reproaching someone for being too modest. And he said, "Let him be, for shyness comes from faith."
It is also narrated in the Ṣaḥīḥayn by ʿImrān Ibn Ḥusayn ﷺ

[130] Māida, 2.

"Modesty brings nothing except good."

It is also narrated in the Ṣaḥīḥayn by Abū Saʿīd al-Khudri ؓ that Rasulullāh ﷺ was more modest than a virgin in her tent. If he disliked something, we knew it from his face."

It is narrated in Ṣaḥīḥ Bukhāri by Abū Masʿūd al-Anṣari ؓ that the Prophet ﷺ said "One of the things which people remember from the time of the early prophecies is the saying that 'If you have no modesty, you might as well do as you wish'."

الْخَامِسُ وَالْخَمْسُونَ من شعب الإيمان

بِرُّ الْوَالِدِينِ لِقَوْلِهِ تَعَالَى ﴿وَوَصَّيْنَا الإِنسَانَ بِوَالِدَيْهِ إِحْسَانًا﴾ وَقَوْلِهِ تَعَالَى ﴿وَقَضَى رَبُّكَ أَلَّا تَعْبُدُوا إِلَّا إِيَّاهُ وَبِالْوَالِدَيْنِ إِحْسَانًا إِمَّا يَبْلُغَنَّ عِنْدَكَ الْكِبَرَ أَحَدُهُمَا أَوْ كِلَاهُمَا فَلَا تَقُل لَّهُمَا أُفٍّ وَلَا تَنْهَرْهُمَا وَقُل لَّهُمَا قَوْلًا كَرِيمًا وَاخْفِضْ لَهُمَا جَنَاحَ الذُّلِّ مِنَ الرَّحْمَةِ وَقُل رَّبِّ ارْحَمْهُمَا كَمَا رَبَّيَانِي صَغِيرًا﴾ الْآيَاتِ.

وَلِحَدِيثِ عَبْدِ اللهِ بْنِ مَسْعُودٍ رَضِيَ اللهُ عَنْهُ فِي الصَّحِيحَيْنِ قَالَ ((سَأَلْتُ النَّبِيَّ صلى الله عَلَيْهِ وَسَلَّمَ أَيُّ الْعَمَلِ أَحَبُّ إِلَى اللهِ عز وجل؟)) قَالَ ((الصَّلَاةُ لَوَقْتِهَا)) قلتُ ((ثُمَّ أَيٌّ؟)) قَالَ ((بِرُّ الْوَالِدَيْنِ)) قلتُ ((ثُمَّ أَيٌّ؟)) قَالَ ((الْجِهَادُ فِي سَبِيلِ اللهِ)) قَالَ ((حَدَّثَنِي بِهِنَّ وَلَوْ اسْتَزَدْتُهُ لَزَادَنِي)).

55. Kindness to parents.

Allāh Taʿālā says: "And to parents do good",[131] and: "We have enjoined upon man, to his parents, good treatment",[132] and: "And your Lord has decreed that you not worship except Him, and to parents, good treatment. Whether one or both of them reach old age [while] with you, say not to them [so much as], 'uff,' and do not

---

[131] Baqara, 83.
[132] Aḥqāf, 15.

repel them but speak to them a noble word. And lower to them the wing of humility out of mercy and say, 'My Lord, have mercy upon them as they brought me up [when I was] small'." [133]
It is also narrated in Ṣaḥīḥayn by Ibn Mas'ūd ﷺ that he asked the Prophet ﷺ "Which action does Allāh Ta'ālā love the most?" and he replied, "Ṣalāt at its time." "And what is next?" I asked, and he said, "Kindness to parents." "And what next?" I enquired, and he replied, "Jihād in the path of Allāh."

السَّادِس وَالْخَمْسُونَ من شعب الإيمان

صلَة الأرحام لقَوْله تَعَالَى ﴿فَهَلْ عَسَيْتُمْ إِنْ تَوَلَّيْتُمْ أن تُفْسِدُوْا فِي الْأَرْضِ وَتُقَطِّعُوْا أرحامَكُمْ أولئك الَّذين لَعَنَهُمُ اللهُ فَأَصَمَّهُمْ وَأَعْمَى أَبْصَارَهُمْ﴾ وَقَوله تَعَالَى ﴿وَالَّذين يَنْقُضُوْنَ عَهْدَ اللهِ مِن بَعْدِ مِيْثَاقِهِ وَيَقْطَعُوْنَ مَا أَمَرَ اللهُ بِهِ أن يُوصَلَ وَيُفْسِدُوْنَ فِي الأَرْضِ أولئك لَهُمُ اللَّعْنَةُ وَلَهُمْ سُوْءِ الدَّارِ﴾.
وَلِحَدِيث أنس بن مَالك رَضِي الله عَنهُ فِي الصَّحِيحَيْنِ ((من أحب أن يبسط لَهُ فِي رزقه وأن ينسأ لَهُ فِي أَثَرِهِ فَليصل رَحمَه)) وَحَدِيث مُحَمَّد بن جُبَير بن مطعم رَضِي الله عَنهُ فيهمَا أيضا عَن أبيه ((لَا يدْخل الْجَنَّة قَاطع)) يَعْنِي قاطع رحم قلت وَلَا فرق بَين أَن يكون برا أَو فَاجِرًا.

56. Maintaining ties of kinship.

Allāh Ta'ālā says: "So would you perhaps, if you turned away, cause corruption on earth and sever your [ties of] relationship? Those [who do so] are the ones that Allāh has cursed, so He deafened them and blinded their vision", [134] and: "Who break the covenant of Allāh after contracting it and sever that which Allāh has ordered

[133] Isrā, 23-24.
[134] Muḥammed, 22-23.

to be joined and cause corruption on earth. It is those who are the losers".[135]

It is narrated in the Ṣaḥīḥayn by Anas ibn Mālik ﵁ that the Prophet ﷺ said, "Whoever would like his sustenance to be increased, and to be blessed in his lifespan, should maintain good ties with his relatives."

It is also narrated in the Ṣaḥīḥayn by the father of Jubayr ibn Mutʿim ﵁ that the Prophet ﷺ said, "No-one who cuts his family ties shall enter the Janna." It makes no difference whether such a person had been good or evil.

السَّابِع وَالْخَمْسُونَ من شعب الإيمان

حسن الْخلق وَيدخل فِيهِ كَظْمُ الغيظِ ولِينُ الْجَانِب والتواضع لقَوْله تَعَالَى ﴿وإنك لعلى خلق عَظِيم﴾ وَقَوله تَعَالَى ﴿والكاظمين الغيظ وَالْعَافِينَ عَن النَّاس وَالله يحب الْمُحْسِنِينَ﴾.

وَلِحَدِيث عبد الله بن عَمْرو رَضِي الله عَنْهُمَا فِي الصَّحِيحَيْنِ أن رَسُول الله صلى الله عَلَيْهِ وَسلم لم يكن فَاحِشا وَلَا متفحشا وَقَالَ ((إن من خياركم أحسنكم أخلاقا))

وَفِي رِوَايَة ((إن من أحبكم إلي أحسنكم أخلاقا)) وَلِحَدِيث عَائِشَة رَضِي الله عَنْهَا فِي الصَّحِيحَيْنِ أيضا أنها قَالَت ((مَا خُيِّرَ رَسُولُ الله صلى الله عَلَيْهِ وَسلم بَين أمرين إلا أَخَذَ أيسرَهُمَا مَا لم يكن إثما. فَإِن كَانَ إثما كَانَ أبعد النَّاس مِنْهُ. وَمَا أنتقم رَسُول الله صلى الله عَلَيْهِ وَسلم لنَفسِهِ إلا أن تنتهك حُرْمَة الله فينتقم لله بهَا)).

وَبِه أنبأنا أبو بكر الْبَيْهَقِيّ، قَالَ: وَمعنى حسن الْخلق: سَلامَة النَّفس نَحْو الأرفق

[135] Baqara, 27.

الأحمد من الْأَفْعَال، وَقد يكون ذَلِك فِي ذَات الله تَعَالَى، وَقد يكون فِيمَا بَين النَّاس، وَهُوَ فِي ذَات الله عز وَجل، أن يكون العَبْد منشرح الصَّدْر بأوامر الله ونواهيه، بِفعل مَا فرض عَلَيْهِ، طيب النَّفس بِهِ سَلِسًا نَحوه. وَيَنْتَهِي عَمَّا حرم عَلَيْهِ، رَاضِيا بِهِ، غير متضجر مِنْهُ، ويرغب فِي نوافل الْخَيْر وَيتْرك كثيرا من الْمُبَاح لوجهه تَعَالَى وتقدس، إذا رأى أن تَركه أقْربُ إلى الْعُبُودِيَّة من فعله مُسْتَبْشِرًا. لذَلِك غير ضجر مِنْهُ، وَلَا متعسر بِهِ، وَهُوَ فِي الْمُعَامَلَات بَين النَّاس، أن يكون سَمحا لحقوقه لَا يُطَالب غَيره بهَا، ويوفي مَا يجب لغيره عَلَيْهِ مِنْهَا. فَإِن مرض وَلم يعد، أَوْ قدم من سفر فَلم يزر، أوْ سلَّم فَلم يرد عَلَيْهِ، أَوْ ضاف فَلم يكرم، أَوْ شفع فَلم يجب، أَوْ أحسن فَلم يشْكر، أَوْ دخل على قوم فَلم يُمكَّن، أوْ تكلم فَلم ينصت لَهُ، أوْ اسْتَأْذن على صديق فَلم يُؤذن لَهُ، أَوْ خطب فَلم يُزَوّج، أوْ أستمهل الدَّين فَلم يُمْهل، أوْ استنقص مِنْهُ فَلم ينقص، وَمَا أشبه ذَلِك، وَلم يغْضب، وَلم يُعَاقب وَلم يتنكر من حَاله حَال، وَلم يستشعر فِي نَفسه أنه قد جُفي وأوحش، وأنه لَا يُقَابل كل ذَلِك إذا وجد السَّبِيل إليه بِمثلِهِ، بل يضمر أنه لَا يعْتد بِشَيْء من ذَلِك، ويقابل كلًّا مِنْهُ بِمَا هُوَ أحسن وأفضل وأقرب إلى الْبرِّ وَالتَّقوى، وأشبه بِمَا يحمد ويرضى، ثمَّ يكون فِي إيفاء مَا يكون عَلَيْهِ، فَهُوَ فِي حفظ مَا يكون لَهُ، فَإِذا مرض أخوه الْمُسلم عَادة، وإن جَاءَ فِي شَفَاعَة شفعه، وإن استمهله فِي قَضَاء دين أمهله، وإن احْتَاجَ مِنْهُ إلى معونته أعانه، وإن استسمحه فِي بيع سمح لَهُ. وَلَا ينظر إلى أن الَّذِي يعامله كَيفَ كَانَت مُعَامَلَته إيّاه فِيمَا خلا، وَكَيف يُعَامل النَّاس، إنّما يتَّخذ الأحسن إمامًا لنَفسِهِ فينحو نَحوه، وَلَا يُخَالِفهُ. والخلق الْحسن قد يكون غريزة، وَقد يكون مكتسبا.

وإنما يَصح اكتسابه مِمَّن كَانَ فِي غريزته أمثل مِنْهُ، فَهُوَ يضم باكتسابه اليه مَا

يتممه.

وَمَعْلُوم فِي الْعَادَات أن ذَا الرأي يزْدَاد بمجالسة أولى الأحلام وَالنَّهْي رأيا. وأن الْعَالم يزْدَاد بمخالطة الْعلمَاء علما. وَكَذَلِكَ الصَّالح. والعاقل بمجالسة الصلحاء والعقلاء. فَلَا يُنكر أن يكون ذُو الْخلق الْجَمِيل يزْدَاد حسن الْخلق بمجالسة أولي الأخلاق الْحَسَنَة. وَبِاللهِ التَّوْفِيق.

57. Good character

This includes suppressing one's anger, and being gentle and humble. Allāh Taʿālā says: "And indeed, you are of a great moral character",[136] and: "who restrain anger and who pardon the people - and Allāh loves the doers of good".[137]

It is narrated in the Ṣaḥīḥayn that ʿAbdullāh ibn ʿAmr ﵁ said: "Rasulullāh ﷺ was never immoderate or obscene. He used to say, 'Among those of you who are most beloved to me are those who have the finest character'."

It is also narrated in the Ṣaḥīḥayn that ʿĀisha ﵂ said, "Never was Rasulullāh ﷺ given the choice between two things except that he chose the easier of them, as long as it entailed no sin. If it did entail sin, he was of all people the most remote from it. Never did he seek revenge for something done against himself; but when the sanctity of Allāh was challenged, he would take vengeance for His sake alone."

The meaning of good character[138] is the inclination of the self towards gentle and praiseworthy acts. This may take place in one's personal actions for Allāh Taʿālā, or in actions which involve other people. In the former case, the slave of Allāh has an open and welcoming heart for His commandments and prohibitions, and

---

[136] Qalam, 4.

[137] Nisā, 134.

[138] The following two pages are reproduced from Shaykh ʿAbdul Hakeem Murad's translation of the *Seventy-Seven branches* of Faith with slight modifications.

does what He has imposed on him happily and easily, and abstains from the things which He has forbidden him with full contentment, and without the least dissatisfaction. He likes to perform optional good acts, and abstains from many permitted things for the sake of Allāh Taʿālā whenever he decides that to abstain in this way would be closer to perfect slavehood to Him. This he does with a contented heart, and without feeling any resentment or hardship. When he deals with other people, he is tolerant when claiming what is his right, and does not ask for anything which is not; but he discharges all the duties which he has towards others. When he falls ill or returns from a trip, and no-one visits him, or when he gives a greeting which is not returned, or when he is a guest but is not honoured, or intercedes but is not responded to, or does a good turn for which he is not thanked, or joins a group of people who do not make room for him to sit, or speaks and is not listened to, or asks permission of a friend to enter, and is not granted it, or proposes to a woman, and is not allowed to marry her, or asks for more time to repay a debt, but is not given more time, or asks for it to be reduced, but is not permitted this, and all similar cases, he does not grow angry, or seek to punish people, or feel within himself that he has been snubbed, or ignored; neither does he try to retaliate with the same treatment when able to do so, but instead tells himself that he does not mind any of these things, and responds to each one of them with something which is better, and closer to goodness and piety, and is more praiseworthy and pleasing. He remembers to carry out his duties to others just as he remembers their duties towards himself, so that when one of his Muslim brethren falls ill he visits him, if he is asked to intercede, he does so, if he is asked for a respite in repaying a debt he agrees, and if someone needs assistance he gives it, and if someone asks for favourable terms in a sale, he consents, all without looking to see how the other person had dealt with him in the past, and to find out how other people behave. Instead, he makes "what is better" the imam of his self, and obeys it completely.

Good character may be something which a man is born with, or it may be acquired. However, it may only be acquired from someone who has it more firmly rooted in his nature than his own. It is well known that a man of sensible opinion can become even more sensible by keeping the company of intelligent and sensible people, and that a learned or a righteous man can learn even more by sitting with other people of learning or righteousness; therefore it cannot be denied that a man of beautiful character may acquire an even more beautiful character by being with people whose characters are superior to his own. And Allāh gives tawfīq!

الثَّامِن وَالْخَمْسُونَ من شعب الإيمان

الإحسان إلى المماليك لقَوْله تَعَالَى ﴿واعبدوا الله وَلَا تُشْرِكُوا بِهِ شَيْئا وبالوالدين إحسانا وبذي القربي واليتامى وَالْمَسَاكِين وَالْجَار ذِي القربي وَالْجَار الْجنب والصاحب بالجنب وَابْن السَّبِيل وَمَا ملكت أيمانكم﴾.

وَلحَدِيث الْمَعْرُور بن سُوَيْد رَضِي الله عَنهُ فِي الصَّحِيحَيْنِ قَالَ ((رأيت أبا ذَر الْغِفَارِيّ رَضِي الله عَنهُ وَعَلِيهِ حلَّة وعَلى غُلَامه حلَّة مثلهَا فَسَأَلْنَاهُ عَن ذَلِك)) فَقَالَ ((إني سابت رجلا)) فَشَكَانِي إِلَى رَسُول الله صلى الله عَلَيْهِ وَسلم فَقَالَ لي رَسُول الله صلى الله عَلَيْهِ وَسلم ((أَعَيَّرْتَهُ بِأُمِّهِ؟! إِنَّكَ امْرُؤٌ فِيْكَ جَاهِلِيَّةٌ)) ثمَّ قَالَ ((إِنَّ إخوانَكُمْ خَوَلُكُمْ جَعَلَهُمُ اللهُ تَحْتَ أَيْدِيكُمْ فَمن كَانَ أَخُوْهُ تحت يَدَيْهِ فَلْيُطْعِمْهُ مِمَّا يَأْكُل وَلْيُلْبِسْهُ مِمَّا يَلْبَس وَلَا تُكَلِّفُوهُمْ من الْعَمَل مَا يَغْلِبهُمْ فَإِن كَلَّفْتُمُوهُمْ مَا يَغْلِبهُمْ فَأَعِينُوهُمْ عَلَيْهِ)).

58. Kindness to bondsmen

Allāh Taʿālā says: "Worship Allāh and associate nothing with Him, and to parents do good, and to relatives, orphans, the needy, the near neighbor, the neighbor farther away, the companion at your side, the traveler, and those whom your right hands possess".[139]

It is narrated in the Ṣaḥīḥayn that Ibn Suwayd said, "I once saw Abū Dhar ؓ with a bondsman of his, and both were wearing identical cloaks. I asked him about this, and he replied, 'I once insulted a man, and he complained of me before Rasulullāh ﷺ, who said to me, "Have you insulted him by his mother? You are a man in whom there is something of the Jahiliyya! Your bondsmen are your brethren, whom Allāh has set in your charge. Whoever has his own brother in his charge must feed him with the food which he eats himself, and clothe him with the clothes which he wears himself, and must not set him excessively hard tasks; in the latter case you must help him yourself'."

التَّاسِع وَالْخَمْسُونَ من شعب الإيمان

حق السَّادة على المماليك وَهُوَ لُزُوم العَبْد سَيِّده وإقامته حَيْثُ يرَاهُ ويأمره بِهِ وطاعته لَهُ فِيمَا يطيقه وَفِي الصَّحِيحَيْنِ من حَدِيث عبد الله بن عمر رَضِي الله عَنْهُمَا أَن رَسُول الله صلى الله عَلَيْهِ وَسلم قَالَ ((أَن العَبْد إذا نصح لسَيِّده وأحسن عبَادَة ربه فَلهُ أجره مرَّتَيْنِ)) وَفِي صَحِيح مُسلم من حَدِيث جرير بن عبد الله رَضِي الله عَنهُ ((أَيما عبد آبق فقد بَرِئت مِنْهُ الذِّمَّة)) وَفِي سنَن أَبِي دَاوُد من حَدِيثه أَيْضا ((العَبْد الآبق لَا يقبل الله مِنْهُ صلَاته حَتَّى يرجع إِلَى موَالِيه)).

59. The rights upon bondsman

It is due right to the master to obey him and fulfill his order according to one's ability. It is narrated in the Ṣaḥīḥayn by 'Abdullāh ibn 'Amr ؓ that Rasulullāh ﷺ said "If the bondsman has good will to his master and worships his Lord perfectly, then he

---

[139] Nisā, 36.

has double reward."
It is narrated in Ṣaḥīḥ Muslim by Jarīr ibn ʿAbdillah ﵁ that Rasulullāh ﷺ said "whenever a bondsman runs away, then he loses his protection". It is narrated in Abū Dāwūd that Rasulullāh ﷺ said "Allāh will not accept ṣalāt from an escaped bondsman until he returns to his master."

السِّتُّونَ من شعب الإيمان

حُقُوق الأولاد والأهلين وَهِي قيام الرجل على وَلَده وأهله وتعليمه إياهم من أمور دينهم مَا يَحْتَاجُونَ إليه لقَوْله تَعَالَى ﴿قوا أنفسكم وأهليكم نَارا وقودها النَّاس وَالْحِجَارَة﴾.

قَالَ الْحسن ((أَي مُرُوهُمْ بِطَاعَة الله وعلموهم الْخَيْر)) وَقَالَ عَلِيّ رَضِي الله عَنهُ ((علِّموهم أدِّبوهم)).

وَلِحَدِيث أنس فِي صَحِيح مُسلم ((من عَال جاريتين حَتَّى تبلغا جَاءَ يَوْم الْقِيَامَة أنا وَهُوَ هَكَذَا وَضم أصبعيه)).

60. The rights of children and family

This consists in a man's looking after his children, and teaching them everything they need to know about their Dīn. Allāh Taʿālā says: "protect yourselves and your families from a Fire whose fuel is people and stones".[140] Hasan al-Baṣri said, regarding this verse, "In other words: command them to obey Allāh, and teach them goodness." ʿAli ﵁ said, "Teach and discipline them."
It is narrated in Ṣaḥīḥ Muslim by Anas ibn Mālik ﵁ that the Prophet ﷺ said "Whoever supports two little girls until they come of age, will be on the Day of Judgement as close to me as this," and

[140] Taḥrīm, 6.

he brought two fingers together.

الْحَادِي وَالسِّتُّونَ من شعب الإيمان

مقاربة أهل الدّين ومودتهم وإفشاء السَّلَام بَينهم والمصافحة لَهُم وَنَحْو ذَلِك من أسباب تَأْكِيد الْمَوَدَّة لقَوْله تَعَالَى ﴿لَا تدْخلُوا بُيُوتًا غير بُيُوتكُمْ حَتَّى تستأنسوا وتسلموا على أهلها﴾.

وَلِحَدِيث أبي هُرَيْرَة رَضِي الله عَنهُ فِي صَحِيح مُسلم ((وَالَّذِي نَفسِي بِيَدِهِ لَا تدخلون الْجنَّة حَتَّى تؤمنوا وَلَا تؤمنوا حَتَّى تحَابوا أ ولا أدلكم على شَيْء إِذا فعلتموه تحاببتم؟ أفشوا السَّلَام بَيْنكُم)) وَحَدِيث قَتَادَة فِي صَحِيح البُخَارِيّ قَالَ ((قلت لأنس رَضِي الله عَنهُ أكانت المصافحة فِي أَصْحَاب النَّبِي صلى الله عَلَيْهِ وَسلم)) فَقَالَ ((نعم)) وَحَدِيث أبي هُرَيْرَة فِي صَحِيح مُسلم ((إِن الله عز وَجل يَقُول يَوْم الْقِيَامَة أَيْنَ المتحابون بجلالي الْيَوْم أظلهم فِي ظِلِّي يَوْم لَا ظلّ إِلا ظِلِّي)).

61. Keeping the company of pious, loving them, greeting them and shaking their hands, and doing any other thing which would strengthen one's affection for them.

Allāh Taʿālā says: "Do not enter houses other than your own houses until you ascertain welcome and greet their inhabitants".[141]
It is narrated in Ṣaḥīḥ Muslim by Abū Hurayra ﷺ that the Prophet ﷺ said, "By Him in Whose hand is my soul, you shall not enter the Janna until you have Imān, and you will not have Imān until you love one another. Shall I tell you of something which, were you to do it, would cause you to love one another? It is to greet the people you meet with salām."

---

[141] Nūr, 27.

It is narrated in Ṣaḥīḥ Bukhari that Qatada said, "I once asked Anas ibn Mālik ﷺ, whether the Companions of the Prophet ﷺ used to shake eachother's hands, and he replied in the affirmative."
It is narrated in Ṣaḥīḥ Muslim by Abū Hurayra ﷺ that the Prophet ﷺ said "On the Day of Qiyama, Almighty Allāh shall declare: 'Where are those who loved one another for My sake, so that I may shade them under My Throne, on a Day when when there will be no shade except My shade?'"

الثَّانِي وَالسِّتُّونَ من شعب الإيمان

ردّ السَّلَام لقَوْله تَعَالَى ﴿وإذا حييتُمْ بِتَحِيَّة فَحَيوا بِأَحْسَن مِنْهَا أَوْ ردوهَا﴾.

وَلِحَدِيث أبي سعيد الْخُدْرِيّ رَضِي الله عَنهُ ((إياكم وَالْجُلُوس فِي الطرقات)) قَالُوا ((يَا رَسُول الله مَا لنا من مجالسنا بُد نتحدث فِيهَا)) فَقَالَ رَسُول الله صلى الله عَلَيْهِ وَسلم ((إذا أبيتم إلا الْمجْلس فأعطوا الطَّرِيق حَقه)) قَالُوا ((وَمَا حق الطَّرِيق؟)) قَالَ ((غض الْبَصَر وكف الأذى ورد السَّلَام والأمر بِالْمَعْرُوفِ وَالنَّهْي عَن الْمُنكر)).

62. Responding to the greetings of others

Allāh Taʿālā says: "When you are greeted with a greeting, greet [in return] with one better than it or [at least] return it [in a like manner]".[142]
It is narrated (in Ṣaḥīḥ Bukhāri) by Abū Saʿīd al-Khudri ﷺ that the Prophet ﷺ said, "You should not sit in the streets." "O Rasulullah!" those present said, "We cannot help it; for we talk to one another there." Rasulullāh ﷺ said, "If you will not refrain, then give the road its rights." "And what are its rights?" they enquired. He

[142] Āl 'Imrān, 86.

replied ﷺ "Lower your gaze, remove obstacles, reply to the salām, enjoin good and forbid evil."

الثَّالِث وَالسِّتُّونَ من شعب الإيمان

عِيَادَة الْمَرِيض لحَدِيث إبْن عَازِب رَضِي الله عَنهُ فِي الصَّحِيحَيْنِ وَسنَن أبي دَاوُد وَغَيرهَا ((أمرنا رَسُول الله صلى الله عَلَيْهِ وَسلم بِسبع ونهانا عَن سبع أمرنا بعيادة المرضى وَاتِّبَاع الْجَنَائِز ورد السَّلَام وتشميت الْعَاطِس وأبرار الْقسم وَنصر الْمَظْلُوم وإجابة الدَّاعِي ونهانا عَن حَلقَة الذَّهَب أَوْ قَالَ خَاتم الذَّهَب وآنية الذَّهَب وَالْفِضَّة والميثرة والقسي والاستبراق وَالْحَرِير والديباج)) وَحَدِيث ثَوْبَان رَضِي الله عَنهُ فِي صَحِيح مُسلم ((عَائِد الْمَرِيض فِي خرفة الْجنَّة حَتَّى يرجع)) قلت وَلَا فرق بَين أن يكون بَرًا اَوْ فَاجِرًا لَكِن ينبسط إلى الْبر وينقبض عَن الْفَاجِر.

63. Visiting the sick

It is narrated in the Ṣaḥīḥayn by Barā' ibn 'Āzib ؓ that Rasulullāh ﷺ commanded us to do seven things i.e. He commanded us to visit the sick, to attend funerals, to reply to the salām of others, to say Allāh have mercy upon you when someone sneezes, to honour one's oath, to help those who are wronged, and to accept invitations."

It is narrated in Ṣaḥīḥ Muslim by Thawbān ؓ that the Prophet ﷺ said, "Whoever visits a sick person will remain in an orchard of Janna until he returns." I say there is no difference in whether the sick is pious or a sinner. However, that Janna is more expansive for the righteous (sick-person) and less so for the sinful.

الرَّابِع وَالسِّتُّونَ من شعب الإيمان

الصَّلَاة على من مَاتَ من أهل الْقبْلَة لحَدِيث أبي هُرَيْرَة رَضِي الله عَنهُ فِي الصَّحِيحَيْنِ ((حق الْمُسلم على الْمُسلم خمس رد السَّلَام وعيادة المرضى وتشميت الْعَاطِس وَاتِّبَاع الْجَنَائِز وإجابة الدعْوَة)) وَحَدِيث ثَوْبَان فِي صَحِيح مُسلم ((من صلى على جَنَازَة فَلهُ قِيرَاط وَمن شهد دَفنهَا فَلهُ قيراطان القيراط مثل أُحدُ)).

64. Praying for any deceased Muslim

It is narrated in the Ṣaḥīḥayn by Abū Hurayra ﵁ that the Prophet ﷺ said, "The Muslim must do these five things: return greetings, visit the sick, say "Allāh have mercy on you," when someone sneezes, attend funerals, and accept invitations."
It is narrated in Ṣaḥīḥ Muslim by Thawbān ﵁ that the Prophet ﷺ said, "Whoever takes part in janāza ṣalāt shall have a qirāṭ, and whoever attends a burial shall have two qirāṭs. A qirāṭ is like Mount Uḥud."

الْخَامِس وَالسِّتُّونَ من شعب الإيمان

تشميت الْعَاطِس لحَدِيث أبي بردة فِي صَحِيح مُسلم عَن أبي مُوسَى الأشعري رَضِي الله عَنهُ قَالَ ((سَمِعت رَسُول الله صلى الله عَلَيْهِ وَسلم يَقُول إِذا عطس أحدكم فحمده الله فشمتوه وإذا لم يحمد الله فَلَا تشمتوه)).

65. Saying "May Allāh have mercy on you!" to someone who sneezes

It is narrated in Ṣaḥīḥ Muslim by Abū Mūsa al-Ashʿari ﵁ that the Prophet ﷺ said, "When one of you sneezes, he should say, 'Praised be Allāh!' and if he does this then the others present should say,

'Allāh have mercy on you!', but if he does not, then they should refrain."

السَّادِس وَالسِّتُّونَ من شعب الإيمان

فِي مباعدة الْكفَّار والمفسدين والغلظة عَلَيْهِم لقَوْله تَعَالَى ﴿لَا يتَّخذ الْمُؤْمِنُونَ الْكَافرين أولياء من دون الْمُؤمنِينَ وَمن يفعل ذَلِك فَلَيْسَ من الله فِي شَيْء إِلَا أن تتقوا مِنْهُم تقاة﴾ وَقَوله تَعَالَى ﴿يَا أَيهَا النَّبِي جَاهد الْكفَّار وَالْمُنَافِقِينَ وَاغْلُظْ عَلَيْهِم﴾ وَقَوله تَعَالَى ﴿قَاتلُوا الَّذين يلونكم من الْكفَّار وليجدوا فِيكُم غلظة﴾ وَقَوله تَعَالَى ﴿يَا أَيهَا الَّذين آمنُوا لَا تَتَّخِذُوا عدوي وَعَدُوكُمْ أولياء تلقونَ إِلَيْهِم بالمودة وَقد كفرُوا بِمَا جَاءَكُم من الْحق يخرجُون الرَّسُول وإياكم أن تؤمنوا بِاللَّه ربكُم إن كُنْتُم خَرَجْتُمْ جهادا فِي سبيلي وابتغاء مرضاتي تسرون اليهم بالمودة﴾ وَقَوله تَعَالَى ﴿يَا ايها الَّذين آمنُوا لَا تَتَّخِذُوا آبَاءَكُم وإخوانكم أولياء أن استحبوا الْكفْر على الإيمان وَمن يَتَوَلَّهُمْ مِنْكُم فَأُولَئِك هم الظَّالِمُونَ﴾ التَّوْبَة ٢٣ الى آخر الاية الَّتِي بعْدهَا وَغَيرهَا من الايات.

وَلِحَدِيث أبي هُرَيْرَة رَضِي الله عَنهُ فِي صَحِيح مُسلم قَالَ رَسُول الله صلى الله عَلَيْهِ وَسلم ((إذا لَقِيتُم الْمُشْركين فِي الطَّرِيق فَلَا تبدؤهم بِالسَّلَامِ واضطروهم إلى أضيقها)) وَحَدِيث أبي سعيد رَضِي الله عَنهُ فِي سنَن أبي دَاوُد ((لَا تصاحب إِلا مُؤمنا وَلَا يَأْكُل طَعَامك إلا تَقِيّ)).

ولهجرة صلى الله عَلَيْهِ وَسلم الثَّلَاثَة الَّذِي خلفوا خمسين يَوْمًا إلى أن تَابَ الله عَلَيْهِم فتابوا وهم كَعْب بن مَالك ومرارة بن الرّبيع وهلال بن أمية رَضِي الله عَنْهُم.

66. Keeping the unbelievers and those who act evilly at a distance, and being stern with them

Allāh Taʿālā says: “Let not believers take disbelievers as allies rather than believers. And whoever [of you] does that has nothing with Allāh, except when taking precaution against them in prudence”,[143] and: “O Prophet, fight against the disbelievers and the hypocrites and be harsh upon them”,[144] and: “O you who have believed, fight those adjacent to you of the disbelievers and let them find in you harshness”,[145] and: “O you who have believed, do not take My enemies and your enemies as allies, extending to them affection while they have disbelieved in what came to you of the truth, having driven out the Prophet and yourselves [only] because you believe in Allāh, your Lord. If you have come out for Jihād in My cause and seeking means to My approval, [take them not as friends]. You confide to them affection, but I am most knowing of what you have concealed and what you have declared. And whoever does it among you has certainly strayed from the soundness of the way. If they gain dominance over you, they would be to you as enemies and extend against you their hands and their tongues with evil, and they wish you would disbelieve”,[146] and: “O you who have believed, do not take your fathers or your brothers as allies if they have preferred disbelief over belief. And whoever does so among you - then it is those who are the wrongdoers”.[147]
It is narrated in Ṣaḥīḥ Muslim by Abū Hurayra ﷺ that the Prophet ﷺ said, “When you meet polytheists in the street, do not greet them first, but force them to walk where it is narrowest.”
It is narrated in Sunan Abū Dawūd by Abū Saʿīd ﷺ that the Prophet ﷺ said: “Only an Allāh fearing person should eat your food, and only a believer should be your companion.”
(An example of such disassociation) is the Prophet’s ﷺ distancing

---

[143] Āl ʿImrān, 28.
[144] Tawba, 73.
[145] Tawba, 123.
[146] Mumtaḥina, 1-2.
[147] Tawba, 23.

from the three who were boycotted for fifty days and who repented and their repentance was accepted. They were Kaʿb bin Mālik, Murāra bin Rabīʿ and Hilāl bin Umayya ﷺ.

السَّابِع وَالسِّتُّونَ من شعب الإيمان

إكرام الجَار لقَوْله تَعَالَى ﴿وبالوالدين إحسانا وبذي الْقُرْبَى واليتامى وَالْمَساكِين وَالْجار ذِي الْقُرْبَى وَالْجار الجُنب والصاحب بالجنب قيل فِي تَفْسِير ذِي الْقُرْبَى الجَار الملاصق وَالْجار الجُنب الْبعيد غير الملاصق والصاحب بالجنب الرفيق فِي السّفر﴾.

وَعَن إبْن عَبَّاس وَمُجاهد وَقَتَادَة والكلبي وَمُقَاتِل بن حَيَّان وَمُقَاتِل بن سُلَيْمَان وَالْجار ذِي الْقُرْبَى الَّذِي بَيْنك وَبَينه قرَابَة وَالْجار الْجنب الأجنبي عَنْك والصاحب بالجنب الرفيق فِي السّفر. وَزَاد مقَاتل بن سُلَيْمَان فَقَالَ فِي الصاحب بالجنب أنه الرفيق فِي السّفر والحضر وَعَن عَليّ وَعبد الله بن مَسْعُود وإبراهيم وَغَيرهم رَضِي الله عَنْهُم فِي الصاحب بالجنب إنها الْمَرْأَة وَعَن سعيد بن جُبَير فِي رِوَايَة كَذَلِك وَفِي رِوَايَة عَنهُ إنه الرفيق الصَّالح. وَالحَدِيث عَائِشَة رَضِي الله عَنْهَا فِي الصَّحِيحَيْنِ أنها سَمِعت رَسُول الله صلى الله عَلَيْهِ وَسلم يَقُول ((مَا زَالَ جِبْرِيل يوصيني بالجار حَتَّى ظَنَنْت انه سيورثه)).

وَبِه أَنبأَنَا الْبَيْهَقِيّ قَالَ أُخْبِرْنَا أبو عبد الله الْحَافِظ فِي مُرَاعَاة حق الرفيق ثَنَا أبو الْعَبَّاس الأصم ثَنَا شُعْبَة عَن عُثْمَان التنوخي ثَنَا مُحَمَّد بن شمال ثنا عبد الرَّزَّاق عَن معمر عَن الزُّهْرِيّ قَالَ قَالَ عبد الله بن عَبَّاس رَضِي الله عَنْهُمَا ((ثَلَاثَة لَا يكافئهم عني إلا رب الْعَالمين: رجل فسح لَهُ فِي مَجْلِسه وَرجل تخطى الْحلق والمجالس حَتَّى جلس الي وَرجل ذكر فِي اللَّيْل حَاجته فرآني اهلا فَكَذَلِك لَا يُكَافِئهُ عني الا رب الْعَالمين)).

67. Honouring one's neighbours

Allāh Taʿālā says: "And to parents do good, and to relatives, orphans, the needy, the near neighbor, the neighbor farther away, the companion at your side, the traveler, and those whom your right hands possess.[148] One interpretation of "the near neighbor" is the neighbour who lives close to you, while "the neighbour who is farther away" refers to a neighbour whose residence is more distant, and the "companion at your side" is a fellow-traveller.
According to Ibn ʿAbbās, Mujāhid, Qatāda, and Muqātil ibn Sulaymān, the "the near neighbor" is he who is related to you, while the "the neighbor farther away" is one who is not. Muqātil added that the "companion at your side" is someone who is one's companion whether on a journey or not.
According to ʿAli رضي الله عنه and Ibn Masʿūd رضي الله عنه, the "companion at your side" refers to one's wife, or, alternatively, to a devout companion.
It is narrated in the Ṣaḥīḥayn by ʿĀishā رضي الله عنها that she heard Rasulullāh ﷺ saying, "So frequently did Jibrīl advise me to be kind to neighbours, that I thought that he would give them a share in one's inheritance."

الثَّامِن وَالسِّتُّونَ من شعب الإيمان

إكرام الضَّيْف لحَدِيث أبي شُرَيْح الْعَدوي رَضِي الله عَنهُ فِي الصَّحِيحَيْنِ قَالَ سَمِعت أذناي وأبصرت عَيْنَايَ حِين تكلم رَسُول الله صلى الله عَلَيْهِ وَسلم فَقَالَ ((من كَانَ يُؤمن بِاللهِ وَالْيَوْم الآخر فَليُكرم ضَيفه جائزته)) قَالُوا ((وَمَا جائزته؟)) قَالَ ((يَوْمه وَلَيْلَته والضيافة ثَلَاثَة أيام فَمَا كَانَ وَرَاء ذَلِك فَهُوَ صَدَقَة عَلَيْهِ)) وَقَالَ ((من كَانَ يُؤمن بِاللهَّ وَالْيَوْم الآخر فَلْيقل خيرا اَوْ ليصمت)) وَزَاد فِي رِوَايَة فِي أوله ((من كَانَ يُؤمن بِاللهِ وَالْيَوْم الآخر فَليُكرم جَاره)).

---

[148] Āl ʿImrān, 36.

68. Honouring guests

It is narrated in the Ṣaḥīḥayn by Abū Shurayḥ ʿAdawi ﵁ that Rasulullāh ﷺ said, "Whoever believes in Allāh and the Last Day must honour his neighbour. Whoever believes in Allāh and the Last Day must honour his guest as he deserves." "And what does he deserve?" he was asked, and he replied, "To be hosted for three days and nights. Anything more is counted as a charity on your part. And whoever believes in Allāh and the Last Day should speak kindly or remain silent."

التاسع والستون من شعب الإيمان

الستر على أصحاب القروف أي الذنوب لقوله تعالى ﴿إنّ الذين يحبون أن تشيع الفاحشة في الذين آمنوا لهم عذاب أليم في الدنيا والآخرة﴾.

ولحديث سالم بن عبد الله بن عمر رضي الله عنهما في الصحيحين عن أبيه ((المسلم أخو المسلم لا يظلمه ولا يسلمه ومن كان في حاجة أخيه كان الله في حاجته ومن فرج عن مؤمن كربه فرج الله عنه بها كربة من كرب يوم القيامة ومن ستر مسلما ستره الله يوم القيامة)).

69. Concealing the sins of others

Allāh Taʿālā says: "Indeed, those who like that immorality should be spread [or publicized] among those who have believed will have a painful punishment in this world and the Hereafter".[149]
It is narrated in the Ṣaḥīḥayn by Ibn ʿUmar ﵁ that Rasulullāh ﷺ said, "A Muslim is a Muslim's brother; he does not wrong or betray him. Whoever aids his brother will be aided by Allāh. And whoever relieves a believer of a trial will be relieved by Allāh of one of the trials of the Day of Reserruction. And whoever conceals the fault

---

[149] Nūr, 19.

of a Muslim will have Allāh conceal his faults on the Day of Reserruction."

السبعون من شعب الإيمان

الصَّبْر على المصائب وَعما تنْزع النَّفس إليه من لذه وشهوة لقَوْله تَعَالَى ﴿وَاسْتَعِينُوا بِالصبرِ وَالصَّلَاة وإنها لكبيرة إلا على الخاشعين﴾ عَن مُجَاهِد وَغَيره أنه أراد بِالصبرِ الصَّوْم وَقَوله تَعَالَى ﴿وَبشر الصابرين الَّذين إِذا أَصَابَتْهُم مُصِيبَة قَالُوا إِنَّا لله وَإِنَّا إِلَيْهِ رَاجِعُون أُولَئِكَ عَلَيْهِم صلوَات من رَبهم وَرَحْمَة وَأُولَئِكَ هم المهتدون﴾ وَقَوله تَعَالَى ﴿إِنَّمَا يُوفى الصَّابِرُونَ أجرهم بِغَيْر حِسَاب﴾ وَغَيرهَا من الْآيَات.

وَالحَدِيث أبي سعيد الْخُدْرِيّ رَضِي الله عَنهُ فِي الصَّحِيحَيْنِ قَالَ جَاءَ أنَاس من الأنصار فسألوا رَسُول الله صلى الله عَلَيْهِ وَسلم فَأَعْطَاهُمْ قَالَ فَجعل لَا يسْأَله أحد مِنْهُم إلا أعطاه حَتَّى نفد مَا عِنْده ثمَّ قَالَ لَهُم حِين أنفق كل شَيْء عِنْده ((مَا يكون عندنَا من خير فَلَنْ ندخره عَنْكُم فَإِنَّهُ من يستعفف يعفه الله وَمن يسْتَغْن يغنه الله وَمن يتصبر يصبره الله وَلنْ تعطوا عَطاء خيرا وأوسع من الصَّبْر)).

وَحَدِيث عبد الله بن مَسْعُود رَضِي الله عَنهُ فيهمَا أيضا قَالَ ((دخلت على رَسُول الله صلى الله عَلَيْهِ وَسلم وَهُوَ يوعك وعكا شَدِيدا)) فَقلت. ((إنك لتوعك وعك الرجلَيْن)) فَقَالَ ((أجل أوعك كَمَا يوعك رجلَانِ مِنْكُم)) قَالَ ((فَقلت ذَلِك بِأَن لَك أَجْرَيْنِ)) قَالَ ((أجل وَمَا من مُسلم يُصِيبهُ أذىً من مرضٍ فَمَا سواهُ إلا حط الله بِهِ من سيئاته كَمَا تحط الشَّجَرَة وَرقهَا)).

70. Steadfastness in the face of misfortunes and against the desires and delights of the ego

Allāh Taʿālā says: "And seek help through patience and prayer, and indeed, it is difficult except for the humbly submissive [to Allāh]".[150] According to Mujāhid and others, "steadfastness" here refers to "fasting". And He has said: "And We will surely test you with something of fear and hunger and a loss of wealth and lives and fruits, but give good tidings to the patient, Who, when disaster strikes them, say, "Indeed we belong to Allāh, and indeed to Him we will return." Those are the ones upon whom are blessings from their Lord and mercy. And it is those who are the [rightly] guided".[151] and: "Indeed, the patient will be given their reward without account".[152]

It is narrated in the Ṣaḥīḥayn by Abū Saʿīd al-Khudri ﷺ that a group of the Ansaar came to Rasulullāh ﷺ assking him for gifts, and, although he gave them what he had, they continued asking until he had nothing left. And when everything had been given to them, he said, "Whenever, I come into possession of something good I will not keep it from you, because whoever is abstinent, shall be helped in this by Allāh, and whoever tries to have no need, Allāh will make him have no needs, and whoever tries to be steadfast Allāh will make him steadfast. No-one is given a gift which is better and more comprehensive than steadfastness."

It is also narrated in the Ṣaḥīḥayn by Ibn Masʿūd ﷺ "I once went to visit Rasulullāh ﷺ when he was very sick. "You have been afflicted with the sickness of two men," I said, and he agreed. "That is because you are to have a two-fold reward," I said. And he told me, "Yes indeed. Whenever a Muslim is afflicted by an illness, or anything else, Allāh strikes out some of his sins, just as a tree sheds its leaves."

---

[150] Baqara, 45.

[151] Baqara, 155-7.

[152] Zumar, 10.

الْحَادِي وَالسَّبْعُونَ من شعب الإيمان

الزّهْد وَقصر الأمل قَوْله تَعَالَى ﴿فَهَل ينظرُونَ إِلَّا السَّاعَة أَن تأتيهم بَغْتَة فقد جَاءَ أشراطها﴾.

وَلِحَدِيث أنس بن مَالك وَسَهل بن سعد رَضِي الله عَنْهُمَا فِي الصَّحِيحَيْنِ ((بُعِثْتُ أَنا والساعة كهاتين وأشار بِأُصْبُعَيْهِ السبابَة وَالْوُسْطَى)) وَحَدِيث إِبْن عَبَّاس رَضِي الله عَنْهُمَا فِي صَحِيح البُخَارِيّ ((نعمتان مغبون فيهمَا كثير من النَّاس الصِّحَّة والفراغ))

وَبِه أَنبأَنَا الْبَيْهَقِيّ قَالَ أنشدني أبو عصمَة مُحَمَّد بن أَحْمَد السجسْتَانِي بِالْبَصْرَةِ لنَفسِهِ فِي هَذَا الْمَعْنى

أَنبأَنَا خير بني آدم ... وَمَا على أَحْمَد إلا الْبَلَاغ

النَّاس مغبونون فِي نعمتي ... صِحَة أبدانهم والفراغ

وَحَدِيث أبي سعيد رَضِي الله عَنهُ فِي صَحِيح مُسلم ((إِنّ الدُّنْيَا حلوة خضرَة وإِنّ الله مستخلفكم فِيهَا فناظر كَيفَ تَعْمَلُونَ فَاتَّقُوا الدُّنْيَا وَاتَّقوا النِّسَاء فَإِن أول فتْنَة إِسرائيل كَانَت فِي النِّسَاء)).

71. Renunciation and curtailing worldly ambitions

Allāh Taʿālā says: "Then do they await except that the Hour should come upon them unexpectedly? But already there have come [some of] its indications".[153]

It is narrated in the Ṣaḥīḥayn by Anas ibn Mālik ﷺ that the Prophet ﷺ said, "I have been sent when the Hour is like this" — and he

[153] Muḥammed, 18.

pointed with his forefinger and middle finger.

It is narrated in Ṣaḥīḥ Bukhari by Ibn ʿAbbās ﵄ that the Prophet ﷺ said, “There are two blessings in which many people are cheated: health and idle-time.” The following couplets were composed by Abū ʿIsma Muḥammed al-Sijistāni of Baṣra:

The best of the descendants of Ādam told us,
and Ahmad had only to inform;
That people are cheated in two blessings:
the health of their bodies, and their spare-time.

It is narrated in Ṣaḥīḥ Muslim by Abū Saʿīd al-Khudri ﵁ that Rasulullāh ﷺ said, “The world is sweet and green (alluring); and verily, Allāh is making you to succeed each other, generations after generations in it in order to see how you act. So, beware of this world and beware of women”.

الثَّانِي وَالسَّبْعُونَ من شعب الإيمان

الْغيرَة وَترك المذاء لقَوْله تَعَالَى ﴿قوا أَنفسكُم وأهليكم نَارا وقودها النَّاس وَالْحِجَارَة﴾ وَقَوله تَعَالَى ﴿وَقل للمؤمنات يغضضن من أبصارهن ويحفظن فروجهن﴾

وَلِحَدِيث أبي هُرَيْرَة رَضِي الله عَنهُ فِي صَحِيح البُخَارِيّ إِنَّ الله عز وَجل يَغَارُ وإِنَّ الْمُؤمنَ يَغَارُ وَغَيْرَةُ اللهِ أن يَأْتِيَ الْمُؤمنُ مَا حَرَّمَ اللهُ عز وَجل عَلَيْه.

وَحَدِيث أم سَلمَة رَضِي الله عَنْهَا فِي الصَّحِيحَيْنِ أن رَسُول الله صلى الله عَلَيْهِ وَسلم كَانَ عِنْدهَا وَفِي الْبَيْت مخنث فَقَالَ لعبد الله بن أبي أمية أخي أم سَلمَة ((يَا عبد الله أن فتح الله لكم الطَّائِف غَدا فَإِنِّي أدلك على إبْنة غيلَان فَإِنَّهَا تقبل بِأَرْبَع وتدبر بثمان)) فَقَالَ رَسُول الله صلى الله عَلَيْهِ وَسلم ((لَا يدْخل هَؤُلَاءِ عَلَيْكُم)).

وَرُوِيَ عَن أبي سعيد الْخُدْرِيّ عَن النَّبِي صلى الله عَلَيْهِ وَسلم أنه قَالَ ((الْغيرَة من الإيمان وإنَّ المِذَاءَ مِنَ النِّفَاق)) قَالَ الْحَلِيمِيّ هُوَ أن يجمع بَين الرِّجَال وَالنِّسَاء ثمَّ يخليهم يماذي بَعضهم بَعْضًا وأخذ من الْمَذْي وَقيل هُوَ إرسال الرِّجَال مَعَ النِّسَاء من قَوْله مذيت الْفرس إذا أرسلتها ترعى.

72. Concern Ghīra (or Ghayra is the sense of jealousy one feels when someone others look at one's wife) for one's family, and not flirting

Allāh Taʿālā says: "Protect yourselves and your families from a Fire whose fuel is people and stones",[154] and: "And tell the believing women to reduce [some] of their vision and guard their private parts".[155]

It is narrated in Ṣaḥīḥ Bukhāri by Abū Hurayra ﵁ that the Prophet ﷺ said, "Allāh is concerned for His preserve, as is the believer. Allāh's concern is that the believer should not approach the forbidden."

It is narrated in the Ṣaḥīḥayn that Umm Salama ﵂ said that the Prophet ﷺ, was once with her, and there was a hermaphrodite in the house, who said to ʿAbdullāh ibn Abi Umayya, the brother of Umm Salama, "ʿAbdullāh! If Allāh allows you to conquer Ṭāʾif tomorrow, I shall take you to the daughter of Ghaylān, who has four rolls of fat in front and eight behind." And Rasulullāh ﷺ said, "These people should not visit you." Abū Saʿīd al-Khudri ﵁ relates that Rasulullāh ﷺ said, "Ghīra is from faith, and flirtation is from hypocrisy."

---

[154] Taḥrīm, 6.

[155] Nūr, 31.

الثَّالِث وَالسَّبْعُونَ من شعب الإيمان

الأعراض عَن اللَّغْو لقَوْله تَعَالَى ﴿قد أفلح الْمُؤْمِنُونَ الَّذين هم فِي صلَاتهم خاشعون وَالَّذين عَن اللَّغْو معرضون﴾ وَقَوله تَعَالَى ﴿وَالَّذين لَا يشْهدُونَ الزُّور وَإِذا مروا بِاللَّغْوِ مروا كراما﴾ وَقَوله تَعَالَى ﴿وَإِذا سمعُوا اللَّغْو أَعرضُوا عَنهُ﴾ واللغو الْبَاطِل الَّذِي لَا يعنيه وَلَا يتَّصل بِقصد صَحِيح وَلَا يكون لقائله فِيهِ فَائِدَة وَرُبمَا كَانَ وبالا عَلَيْهِ.

وَفِي حَدِيث أبي سَلمَة عَن أبي هُرَيْرَة وَعلي بن الْحُسَيْن عَن أبيه عَن عَليّ رَضِي الله عَنْهُم أن رَسُول الله صلى الله عَلَيْهِ وَسلم قَالَ ((من حسن إسلام الْمَرْء تَركه مَا لَا يعنيه)) وَبِه أَنبأَنَا الْبَيْهَقِيّ أَنبأَنَا أبو عبد الله الْحَافِظ ثَنَا الْحسن بن مُحَمَّد بن إسحاق قَالَ سَمِعت أبا عُثْمَان الحناط قَالَ سَمِعت ذَا النُّون يَقُول:

من حب الله عَاشَ وَمن مَال إِلَى غَيره طاش
والأحمق يَغْدُو وَيروح فِي لاش والعاقل عَن خواطر نَفسه فتاش

73. Turning away from pointless talk

Allāh Taʿālā says: "Certainly will the believers have succeeded: They who are during their prayer humbly submissive. And they who turn away from ill speech".[156] and: "And [they are] those who do not testify to falsehood, and when they pass near ill speech, they pass by with dignity",[157] and: "And when they hear ill speech, they turn away from it".[158]
'Pointless talk' (laghw) is speech which is futile and irrelevant, and bears no relation to any true purpose. It brings no benefit to the one who utters it, and may well bring him misfortune instead.

---

[156] Mu'minūn, 1-3.
[157] Furqān, 72.
[158] Qaṣaṣ, 55.

'Ali ؓ related that Rasulullāh ﷺ said, "It is part of a man's sound practice of Islam that he leaves alone that which is of no concern to him."

Dhun-Nūn said:
> Whoever loves Allāh lives truly,
> and whoever inclines to anything else damages his mind.
> A foolish man comes and goes, paying attention to what is nothing,
> while the intelligent man inspects his own thoughts scrupulously.

الرَّابِعُ وَالسَّبْعُونَ مِن شعب الإيمان

الجُودُ والسخاء لقَوْلِه تَعَالَى ﴿وسارعوا إلى مغفرة من ربكم وجنة عرضها السَّمَوَات والارض أعدت لِلْمُتَّقِين الَّذِين يُنْفِقُونَ فِي السرَّاءِ وَالضَّرَّاءِ﴾ وَغَيْرهَا من الآيات وَقَوْله تَعَالَى فِي عَكسه ﴿الَّذِين يَبْخلُونَ ويأمرون النَّاس بالبخل ويكتمون مَا آتَاهُم الله من فَضله وأعتدنا لِلْكَافرِينَ عذَابا مهينا﴾ وَقَوله تَعَالَى ﴿وَمن يبخل فَإِنَّمَا يبخل عَن نَفسه﴾ وَقَوله تَعَالَى ﴿وَمن يُوقَ شح نَفسه فَأُولَئِك هم المفلحون﴾ وَغَيرهَا من الآيات.

وَلِحَدِيث أَبِي هُرَيْرَة رَضِي الله عَنهُ فِي الصَّحِيحَيْنِ ((مَا من يَوْم يصبح الْعباد فِيهِ إلا ملكان ينزلان فَيَقُول أحدهما اللَّهُمَّ أعط منفقا خلفا وَيَقُول الآخر اللَّهُمَّ أعط ممسكا تلفا)).

74. Generosity and benevolence

Allāh Ta'ālā says: "And hasten to forgiveness from your Lord and a garden as wide as the heavens and earth, prepared for the righteous, who spend [in the cause of Allāh] during ease and hardship",[159] and: "Who are stingy and enjoin upon [other] people stinginess and conceal what Allāh has given them of His bounty - and We have prepared for the disbelievers a humiliating

---

[159] Āl 'Imrān, 133.

punishment”,[160] and: “but among you are those who withhold [out of greed]. And whoever withholds only withholds [benefit] from himself”,[161] and: “And whoever is protected from the stinginess of his soul - it is those who will be the successful”.[162]
It is narrated in the Ṣaḥīḥayn by Abū Hurayra ﷺ that the Prophet ﷺ said, “Every morning two angels descend, one of whom says, ‘O Lord Allāh! Bless the posterity of him who spends!’ and the other, ‘O Lord Allāh! Destroy him who withholds!’”

الْخَامِس وَالسَّبْعُونَ من شعب الإيمان

رحم الصَّغِير وتوقير الْكَبِيرلحَدِيث جرير بن عبد الله فِي صَحِيح مُسلم من لَا يرحم النَّاس لَا يرحمه الله تَعَالَى.

وَحَدِيث أبي هُرَيْرَة رَضِي الله عَنهُ فِي الصَّحِيحَيْنِ ((جعل الله الرَّحْمَة مائَة جُزْء فَأمْسك عِنْده تِسْعَة وَتِسْعين جُزْءا وَانْزِلْ فِي الأَرْض جُزْءا وَاحِدًا فَمن ذَلِك الْجُزْء يتراحم الْخَلَائق حَتَّى ترفع الْفرس حافرها عَن وَلَدهَا خشيَة أن تصيبه)).

وَحَدِيث عبد الله بن عَمْرو رَضِي الله عَنْهُمَا فِي سنَن أبي دَاوُد وَمُسلم ((من لم يرحم صَغِيرنَا وَلم يعرف حق كَبِيرنَا فَلَيْسَ منا)).

وروينا فِي الصِّحَاح فِي حَدِيث الْقسَامَة كبر الْكبر أَوْ الْكبر الْكبر أَي يتَكَلَّم أكبركم وَفِي حَدِيث الإمامة ((وليؤمكم أكبركم)).

75. To have mercy for the young and respect for the old

It is narrated in Ṣaḥīḥ Muslim by Jarīr ibn ʿAbdullāh ﷺ that the Prophet ﷺ said, “Allāh will not have mercy for him who does not have mercy for others.”

---

[160] Nisā, 37.
[161] Muḥammed, 38.
[162] Ḥashr, 9.

It is narrated in the Ṣaḥīḥayn by Abū Hurayra ﷺ that the Prophet ﷺ said, "Allāh has divided mercy into a hundred parts, ninety-nine of which has He withheld, sending the other down upon the earth. Whenever His creatures show mercy to one another it is through this one part, even when a mare is fearful of treading on her foal."
It is narrated in Ṣaḥīḥ Muslim and Abū Dawūd by ʿAbdullāh ibn ʿAmr ﷺ that the Prophet ﷺ said, "Whoever does not show mercy to our young, and does not know the rights of our elders, is not one of us."
In the ḥadīth of all the Ṣiḥāḥ (six most authentic ḥadīth texts) it is related that "Give priority to the most senior" i.e. the most senior should speak on behalf of your group.
In the ḥadīth of imamate it is related (by Bukhāri and Muslim), "Your imām should be the most senior among you."

السَّادِس وَالسَّبْعُونَ من شعب الإيمان

إصلاح ذَات الْبَين لقَوْله تَعَالَى ﴿لَا خير فِي كثير من نَجوَاهُمْ إلا من أمْر بِصَدقَة اَوْ مَعْرُوف اَوْ إصلاح بَين النَّاس وَمن يفعل ذَلِك ابْتِغَاء مرضات الله فَسَوف نؤتيه أجرا عَظِيما﴾ وَقَوله تَعَالَى ﴿إنما الْمُؤْمِنُونَ إخوة فأصلحو بَين أخويكم أَي بَين كل اثْنَيْنِ مِنْكُم﴾.

وَالحَدِيث أم كُلْثُوم بنت عقبَة بن أبي معيط رَضِي الله عَنْهَا فِي الصَّحِيحَيْنِ ((لَيْسَ الْكذَّاب الَّذِي يصلح بَين النَّاس فَيَقُول خيرا وينمي خيرا)) قَالَت ((وَلم أسْمَعْهُ يرخص فِي شَيْء مِمَّا يَقُول النَّاس كذبا إلا فِي ثَلَاث الْحَرْب والإصلاح بَين النَّاس وَحَدِيث الرجل إمراته وَحَدِيث المراة زَوجهَا)).

76. Reconciling people's differences

Allāh Taʿālā says: "No good is there in much of their private conversation, except for those who enjoin charity or that which is right or conciliation between people. And whoever does that seeking means to the approval of Allāh - then We are going to give him a great reward".[163] and: "The believers are but brothers, so make settlement between your brothers".[164]

It is narrated in the Ṣaḥīḥayn by Umm Kulthūm bint ʿUqba رضي الله عنها that Rasulullāh ﷺ said, "He is not a liar who makes peace between people, saying what is good and not mentioning what is dishonourable." And she said, "I never heard him permitting any kind of lying, except with regard to three things: war, reconciling people's differences, and what a man says to his wife, and what a wife says to her husband."

السَّابِع وَالسَّبْعُونَ من شعب الإيمان

أن يحب الرجل لأخيه الْمُسلم مَا يحب لنَفسِهِ وَيَكرَهُ لَهُ مَا يَكرَه لنَفسِهِ.

وَيدخل فِيهِ إماطة الاذى عَن الطَّرِيق الْمشَار إليه فِي حَدِيث أبي هُرَيْرَة رَضِي الله عَنهُ فِي الصَّحِيحَيْنِ ((الإيمان بضع وَسِتُّونَ أَوْ بضع وَسَبْعُونَ شُعْبَة أفضلها قَول لَا إله إلا الله وَأَدْنَاهَا إماطة الأذى عَن الطَّرِيق وَالْحيَاء شُعْبَة من الإيمان)).

وَحَدِيث أنس فِي صَحِيح البُخَارِيّ ((لَا يُؤمن أحدكم حَتَّى يحب لأخيه مَا يحب لنفسِهِ)). وَحَدِيث جرير بن عبد الله فِي الصَّحِيحَيْنِ بَايَعتُ رَسُولَ الله صلى الله عَلَيْهِ وَسلّم على إقام الصَّلَاة وإيتاء الزَّكَاة والنُّصْحِ لكل مُسلم.

77. To love for your Muslim brother what you love for yourself, and to hate for him what one would hate for yourself

This includes the "removal of something harmful from a road" referred to in the ḥadīth of Abū Hurayra رضي الله عنه reported in the Ṣaḥīḥayn: "Īmān has sixty-odd, or seventy-odd, branches, the

---

[163] Nisā, 114.

[164] Muḥammed, 10

highest and best of which is to declare that *Lā-ilāha il-lal-lāhu (there is none worthy of worship except Allāh)*, and the lowest of which is to remove something harmful from a road. Shyness, too, is a branch of Īmān."

It is narrated in Ṣaḥīḥ Bukhāri by Anas ﷺ that the Prophet ﷺ said, "None of you have Īmān until he wishes for his brother that which he wishes for himself."

It is narrated in the Ṣaḥīḥayn by Jarīr bin ʿAbdullāh ﷺ that the Prophet ﷺ said, "I pledged my allegiance to Rasulullāh ﷺ with the undertaking that I would observe ṣalāt, pay the zakāt, and have goodwill to every Muslim."

تم الكتاب والحمد لله أولا وآخرا

Here the book is completed and all praises are due to Allāh at the beginning and the end.

Poem on the Branches of Imān

By Imām Zayn ud Dīn Malabāri رَحِمَهُ ٱللَّهُ

بسم الله الرحمن الرحيم

In the name of Allāh the most Beneficent and merciful

اَلْحَمْدُ لِلّٰهِ الَّذِى قَدْ صَيَّرَا إِيْمَانَ شَخْصٍ ذَا شُعَبْ فَتُتَمَّمْ
هَذِىْ بُيُوْتٌ مِنْ كِتَابِ الْكُوْشِنِي مَنْ قَالَ بَعْدَ صَلاَتِنَا نُسَلِّمُ
لِمُحَمَّدٍ وَلِآلِهِ وَصَحَابَتِهْ مَادَارَ شَمْسٌ فِي السَّمَاءِ وَأَنْجُمُ

All praise is due to Allāh who completed
imān of a person into many branches.
These verses are from the writings of Al-Kūshinī
Who said after our peace and blessings,
Upon Muḥammed and his househand and companions
As long as the sun and the stars are orbiting in the sky

إِيْمَانُنَا بِضْعٌ وَعَيْنٌ شُعْبَةً يَسْتَكْمِلَنْهَا اَهْلُ فَضْلٍ يَعْظُمُ

Our Imān is a an odd-few and certain (seventy) branches
The virtuous surely seek to complete these (in themselves) and become great.

آمِنْ بِرَبِّكَ وَالْمَلاَئِكِ وَالْكُتُبِ وَالأَنْبِيَا وَبِيَوْمٍ يَفْنَى لْعَالَمُ

Have belief in your Lord, the angels, the books,
The Prophets and a Day when the world will end.

وَالْبَعْثِ وَالْقَدَرِ الْجَلِيْلِ وَجَمْعِنَا فِي مَحْشَرٍ فِيهِ الْخَلاَئِقُ تَحْشَمُ

And the reserruction, the imposing pre-ordainment, our coming together.
In the Great Gathering Ground in which the creation feels ashamed

وَاحْبُبْ اِلَهَكَ خَفْ اَلِيْمَ عِقَابِهِ   وَلِرَحْمَةِ ارْجُ تَوَكَّلَنْ يَا مُسْلِمُ

And love your God and fear his painful torment
And hope of his Mercy and rely upon Him, O Muslim.

وَاحْبُبْ نَبِيَّكَ ثُمَّ عَظِّمْ قَدْرَهُ   وَابْخِلْ بِدِيْنِكَ مَا يُرَى بِكَ مَأْثَمُ

And love your Prophet and revere his rank
Be prudent in your deen, so no sin becomes apparent from you.

وَاطْلُبْ لِعِلْمٍ ثُمَّ لَقِّنْهُ الْوَرَى   عَظِّمْ كَلاَمَ الرَّبِّ وَاطْهُر تُعْصَمُ

And seek knowledge and then teach it to mankind
Revere the Lord's speech and purify so you may become sinless

صَلِّ الصَّلاَةَ وَزَكِّ مَالَكَ ثُمَّ صُمْ   وَاعْكُفْ وَحُجَّ وَجَاهِدَنَّ فَتُكْرَمُ

Pray your Ṣalāt and give your Zakāt on your wealth and fast
Make Iʿtikāf, Ḥajj and Jihād so you maybe honoured.

رَابِطْ تَثَبَّتْ اَدِّ خُمْسَ مَغَانِمٍ   حَتَّى يُفَرِّقَهُ الإِمَامُ الْحَاكِمُ

Protect the borders and be firm-footed and give the the khums of the spoils of war
Until the ruling leader distributes it

وَاعْتِقْ وَكَفِّرْ اَوْفِ بِالْوَعْدِ اشْكُرَنْ   وَاحْفَظْ لِسَانَكَ ثُمَّ فَرْجَكَ تَغْنَمُ

Free the slaves, pay expiations, honour agreements and be Grateful
And protect your tongues and private-parts, so you may prosper

اَدِّ اْلاَمَانَةَ لاَ تُقَاتِلْ مُسْلِمًا   وَاحْذَرْ طَعَامًا ثُمَّ مَالَكَ تَحْرُم

Fulfill the safe-keeping and do not kill any Muslim
Be cautious of ḥarām in your food and also your wealth

وَالزِّيَّ مَعْ ظَرْفٍ وَلَهْوًا قَدْ نُهِيْ   اَنْفِقْ بِمَعْرُوْفٍ وَإِلاَّ تَأْثَمُ

Beware of forbidden attire, vessels and amusements
Spend in good else you will sin.

اُتْرُكْ وَاَمْسِكْ كُلَّ غِلٍّ وَالْحَسَدَ   حَرِّمْ لِعِرْضِ الْمُسْلِمِيْنَ فَتَسْلَمُ

Leave and keep away rancour and jealousy
Consider the honour of the Muslims forbidden and you will be safe

أَخْلِصْ لِرَبِّكَ ثُمَّ سُرَّ بِطَاعَةٍ   وَاحْزَنْ بِسُوْءٍ تُبْ وَاَنْتَ النَّادِمُ

Be sincere to your Lord and be joyous on his obedience
Grieve on wickedness and repent while you are regretful.

وَائْتِ الضَّحِيَّةَ وَالْعَقِيْقَةَ وَاهْدِيَنْ   وَاُولِى الاُمُوْرِاَطِعْهُمُ لاَتَجْرِمُ

Offer the sacrifice (at ʿĪd), aqīqa and sacrifice (at Ḥajj)
Those in authority (rulers, commanders and ʿulamā) should be obeyed and not rebelled.

اَمْسِكْ حَبِيْبِى مَا عَلَيْهِ جَمَاعَةٌ   وَاحْكُمْ بِعَدْلٍ وَانْهَ مَاهُوَ مَأْثَمُ

Stick to the main body of the Muslims O my beloved.
Judge with justice and prevent sins.

وَأْمُرْ بِمَعْرُوْفٍ وَاَنْتَ اَعِنْهُمْ   جِدًّا عَلَى بِرٍّ وَتَقْوَى تُـكْرَمُ

Enjoin the good and aid its enjoiners
Much towards righteousness and taqwa and you will be honoured.

وَاسْتَحْيِ رَبَّكَ اَحْسِنَنْ لِلْوَالِدِ   رَحِمًا فَصِلْ حَسِّنْ بِخُلْقِكَ تُرْحَمُ

Feel shame before your Lord and certainly be kind to your father
As for family ties, strengthen them and have good akhlāq with the creation and mercy will be shown to you.

اَحْسِنْ لِقِنِّكَ فَاعْفُ عَنْهُ وَعَلِّمَنْ   وَاِطَاعَةُ السَّادَاتِ عَبْدًاتَلْزَمُ

Be kind to your slave and overlook their faults and teach them.
Obedience to masters by a slave is obligatory.

وَاحْفَظْ حُقُوْقَ الاَهْلِ وَالاَوْلَادِ   اَنْفِقْ وَعَلِّمْهُمْ فَذَاكَ مُحَـتَّمُ

Guard the rights of your household and children.
Spend upon them and teach them that is ordained.

وَاحْبُبْ لأَهْلِ الدِّيْنِ رُدَّ سَلاَمَهُمْ   عُوْدَنَّ مَرْضَى صَلِّ مَوْتَى أَسْلَمُوْا

Love the people of dīn and reply to their salām
Visit the sick and pray upon the deceased Muslims.

شَمِّتْ لِعَاطِشٍ مُسْلِمٍ حَمِدَ الْإِلَهَ   وَابْعُدْ اَخِي عَنْ مُفْسِدٍ لاَتُظْلَمُ

Reply to the Muslim who says Alḥamdulillah after sneezing.
And be distant from what corrupts, O brother and do not oppress.

اَكْرِمِ لِجَارٍ ثُمَّ ضَيْفٍ وَاسْتُرَنْ   عَوْرَاتِ اَهْلِ الدِّيْنِ تَأْمَنْ تَغْنَمُ

Honour your neighbor and your guest and conceal
The faults of people of dīn and you will be safe and will prosper.

وَاصْبِرْ تَزَهَّدْ وَائْتِيَنَّ بِغِيْرَةٍ   اَعْرِضْ عَنْ الْمَلْغَاةِ جُدْ تَتَكَرَّمُ

Be patient and have indifference (to the world) and have ghīra
Turn away from frivolous pursuits and strive and you will be honoured.

وَقِّرْ كَبِيْرًا وَارْحَمَنَّ صَغِيْرَنَا   أَصْلِحْ لِهَجْرِ الْمُسْلِمِيْنَ فَتُكْرَمُ

Revere elders and have mercy on the young.
Reconcile after cutting-off relations and you will be honoured.

وَاحْبُبْ لِنَاسٍ مَا تُحِبُّ لِنَفْسِكَ   حَتَّى تَكُوْنَ بِجَنَّةٍ تَتَنَعَّمُ

Love for people what you love fo your self.
So that you can relish the pleasures Janna.

Our Publications

Ḥanbali Fiqh of Worship

Mukhtaṣarul Ḥizbul Aʿẓam

The Branches of Īmān

Firdaws Academy Press